GHOST TOWNS AND LOCATIONS
OF THE MESABI IRON RANGE

By Rod Halunen

Written in 1966 in fulfillment
for a Master's Degree from the
University of Minnesota

Reproduced in celebration of
the centennial year
1992

Range Printing, Virginia, MN

DEDICATED TO OUR
COURAGEOUS PIONEER
ANCESTORS.

ACKNOWLEDGEMENTS

I gratefully acknowledge the following who have generously given of their time and energy and provided information which aided me in the completion of this book:

Matt Viitala, Mrs. Emil Anttila, Harvey Terrio, Anton Cerkvenik, Andrew Saari, Joe Squillace Sr., Saunder Lawrence, George Raukar, George Chanak, Mrs. Paul Kochar, Molly Cavanaugh, Joe Milinovich, Mrs. E.S. Tillinghast, Helmi Bergdahl, Cico Gentilini, George Anderson, William Turja, Helen Skarp, Andrew Benkusky, George Lohneis, Esther "Terry" Haapala, Pete Hansen Jr., Tito Gianlorenzi Sr., Mrs. E.M. Moline, Ed Mills, Bill Kaiser, Hulda Hammer, Horton Peterson, John Thomas, William Zacher, Etta Young, Grace Zacher Woods, Carl Lawry, Anton Kohlroser, Mrs. Elmer Makinen, Mrs. Ray Ferrey, Jessie Grierson, Mrs. Fred Brown, Jack Heiska, Peter Volden, Siguard Copperud, Ed Norsted, Gust Erickson, Harry Bernicke, George Dobbs, Violet Nakari, Franklin King, Heinie Michelson, Charles Shubat, Don Hildreth, John Krasaway, Secundo Muscatelli, Sam Trebilcock, Rolland Stickney and Jim O'Leary. Also, the Mesabi Daily News, Duluth News Tribune, Hibbing Daily News, Eveleth News Clarion, St. Louis Historical Society, Minnesota Historical Society, Virginia Public Library, Eveleth Public Library, Duluth Public Library, Hibbing Public Library and Mt. Iron Public Library. Special Appreciation is given to the late, Dr. Maude Lindquist, Head, History Department, University of Minnesota, Duluth.

I further wish to express sincere appreciation to my wife, Mary Lou, who helped me from beginning to end of this publication.

Cover design by our son, Todd.

PREFACE

Northern Minnesota lay wild and dense for centuries before white man had set foot in it. Early Indians, the Sioux and Chippewas, hunted and fished with leisure and complacency without fear of human enemies. In time, white explorers and missionaries began charting lands along the Mississippi, St. Lawrence, and Pidgeon Rivers. News of the great wealth of Minnesota soon spread. About 1800, white-man began building fur trading posts at such places as Duluth, Pidgeon Falls, and Grand Portage. French lumber barons soon recognized the tremendous fortune in the un-touched virgin forests.

In the late 1800's, iron bearing rock was discovered in the Tower Soudan region. There was speculation con-cerning the great wealth that lay beneath Northern Minn-esota's topsoil, but all was forgotten in the "gold fever" of 1865 when gold was discovered in the Vermillion Range. The greatest significance of this discovery is the probable hastening of the time when iron mines would be developed bringing up the Vermillion Trail; rugged teamsters singing "cousin jacks," boisterous lumberjacks, hardy cruisers, prospectors, railroad men, old-time politicians, pioneer doctors, and such mining men as Munro, Longyear, Bennett, Hartley, Alworth, Agnew, and the Merritts.

Towns mushroomed overnight populated by people of various nationalities who had come to this country in search of a better life. Some of these towns and cities prospered, others whithered and died, leaving rotting remnants of homes, stores, and stables.

The following pages will tell the story of the life and death of some of these mining communities, once known to many but now living only in the memories of a few.

Outline of Contents

-I-

MAP OF MESABI IRON RANGE

MESABA RANGE

ST. LOUIS COUNTY

LAKE SUPERIOR

▨ — Ghost Towns + Loc.

-II-

IRON JUNCTION, AN EARLY RAILROAD
GHOST TOWN

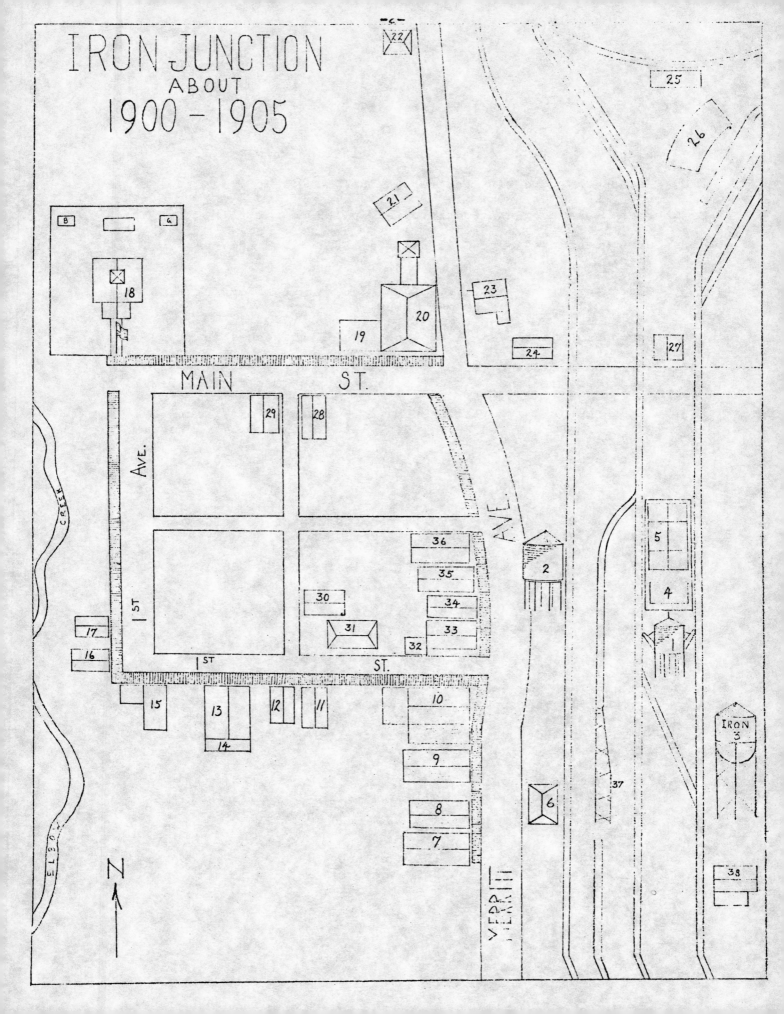

IRON JUNCTION
ABOUT
1900 - 1905

KEY TO MAP OF IRON JUNCTION   (about 1900-1905)

1. First water tank   (Constructed in 1894 of wood)

2. Second water tank   (Constructed in 1901 of wood)

3. Present water tank   (Constructed in 1929 of metal)

4. Cafe owned by George Collins, Mrs. C. Carlson and Mrs. T. C. Young

5. Depot for D. M. & N. Ry.   (T. C. Young, second operator lived with his family in the apartment above depot)

6. Warehouse built by E. M. Moline in 1915 and razed in 1939

7. Residence of Clark Pierson and later owned by J. A. Grierson and family who was the bridge construction foreman for the railroad

8. Residence of Charles Klingensmith, postmaster and grocer followed by John McKaige, Dan Perry, Mrs. Etta Young and E. M. Moline

9. Store owned by Klingensmith, McKaige, Perry, and Moline

10. M. R. Johnson store

11. Residence of Mr. and Mrs. Larson (Carpenter on bridge and building crew, later used for storage by Moline store)

12. Residence of J. R. Gillis and family (Later used for storage by Moline store)

13. Village Hall and jail (Later a restaurant, barbershop used by Albert Fischer and now a cabinet shop)

14. Three room jail with Dan Perry as constable

15. Granary (No. 30) was moved to this lot and remodeled by Dan Shoven. It was occupied by Steve Ryan and family.

16. Steam operated pump which kept water tanks full for use in engines and by fire department

17. First gasoline operated pump on D. M. & N. Ry. Ed McDonald suffered fatal injuries while inspecting the pump while it was in motion. Pumper Love was killed by same pump while trying to start it.

18. Schoolhouse District 25 (Discontinued use about 1939 by action taken by County Board in that year. Arthur Lampe was Superintendent.

19. Barroom of the Downey Hotel owned by Dixon and Laury of Duluth and managed by Bob Downey Sr.

20. Three story Downey Hotel (Privvy for each floor located at rear of building)

21. Residence of Mr. and Mrs. McQuade and family (They moved out in 1897)

22. Residence of Mr. and Mrs. "Paddie" Fitzpatrick

23. Section house for section foreman Charles F. Zacher and family from 1897-1912

24. Hand car house

25. Bridge and building shop

26. Two stall roundhouse

27. Tent restaurant operated and owned by Mr. and Mrs. E. B. Perry

28. Vacant saloon building which was later occupied by Mr. and Mrs. Eric Frautsi

29. Vacant saloon (Remained vacant until razed)

30. Granary owned by Frank Ansley

31. Barn owned by Frank Ansley

32. Town well (Located in Room behind Frank Ansley Saloon)

33. Frank Ansley Saloon (Also sometimes called "Stoney Brook Saloon")

34. Vacant saloon

35. August Carlson Saloon

36. Missabe Hotel owned and managed by M. R. Johnson

37. Coal dock for refueling engines

38. Residence of Mr. and Mrs. Dougal

IRON JUNCTION

In the summer of 1890, towering Jack Pine gave way to railroad tracks which connected the port of Duluth with Mountain Iron and Biwabik, and the subsequent junction, in time, was destined to become one of the fastest growing, liveliest towns on the Iron Range. The Duluth, Missabe and Northern (D. M. & N.) Railroad built a two stall roundhouse, rip-track and depot which was proof that the firm recognized the future importance of the town as a railroad intersection, and the town of Iron Junction was born. Talk was running high that the railroad Company was considering building a larger roundhouse,

IRON JUNCTION, ABOUT 1905

expanding the coal docks, increasing the number of section houses and developing the area as a maintenance and refueling center. Things started to "boom." A sudden influx of people hoped to become a part of the new city that in only a few months had built many homes, thirteen saloons, four hotels, shops and stores. [1] By

1. Young, Mrs. Etta Young, resident of Iron Junction, Minnesota, from 1897-1920, letter dated April 4, 1965

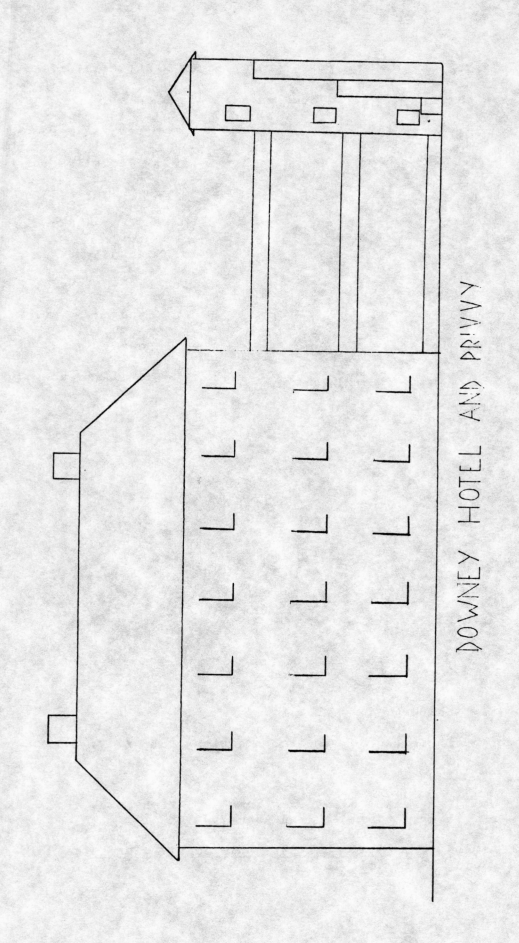

DOWNEY HOTEL AND PRIVVY

1893, there were one hundred forty-two legal voters in the village of a total population of three hundred sixty-five. [2]

DOWNEY HOTEL, IRON JUNCTION

The railroad men were supporting the large thirty-room Downey Hotel which was owned by Dixon and Laury of Duluth and managed by Mr. Bob Downey, and the Hotel Missaba, owned by Mr. M.R. Johnson, and two others. [3] Offices of dispatcher H.M. Eskelman who controlled train movements for the entire road, the master mechanic A. F. Priest who was in charge of the mechanics department, the

TEN CAR COAL DOCK, IRON JUNCTION

roadmaster Fred Davis and the general storekeeper E. A. W. Brick were

2. Zacher, William, resident of Iron Junction, Minnesota, from 1897-1909, interview of July and August, 1965

3. Van Brunt, Walter, Duluth and St. Louis County Minnesota (Chicago and New York, 1921) Vol. II

then located in the junction city. 4

(1)   (2)   (3)   (4)   (5)   (6)

(7)

(8)   (10)   (11)

(9)   (15)

(12)   (13)   (14)   (16)

(1) Eric Strand - - worked in the saloons as a helper
(2) Bob Downey, Jr. - - son of hotel owner
(3) "Blackie" - - transient
(4) Steve Ryan - - owner of the property railroad wanted to buy
(5) John McKeig - - railroad's Bridge and Building Department
(6) Bob Downey - - hotel owner
(7) Mr. Sullivan - - ran a hotel in log cabin east of depot. He
                    had neither teeth nor hair and always wore a
                    hat.
(8) Charles Zacher - - section foreman
(9) Sam Riando - - bartender for Frank Ansley
(10) Neil MacIntoch - - Pumper railroad
(11) M. R. Johnson - - storekeeper, postmaster and hotel owner
(12) Albert Fisher - - coal dock tender
(13) George Patterson - - railroad's Bridge and Building Department
(14) Frank Ansley - - saloon keeper
(15) Thomas Young - - station agent
(16) Herb Shores - - lumberman

(these sixteen men took a hand car to Eveleth one Sunday just to
have this picture taken.)

----

4. "Seventy Years at Iron Junction", Missabe Iron Ranger, October
    1962

A petition to incorporate was circulated in May 1893, by
John Campbell, Frank Ansley, Stephen Ryan, Sam Riando, M. R. Johnson, George Patterson, Herb Shores and a Mr. Sullivan. [5] With
a total of four hundred eighty acres involved in the village
corporate powers, this was deemed "regular" by the St. Louis
County Board of Commissioners, who ordered an election to be
held on July 25, 1893 "at the store building of P. J. Clure."

HOTEL MISSABE

One hundred and forty-two unanimous votes were for incorporation whereupon, the commissioners
ordered election for officers to
be held on August 10, "in the
vacant building near the P. J.
Clure store." [6] Ryan Junction,
as it was then called, was
renamed Iron Junction because
of its strategic position. In
the next seven decades, the
"red rust" handled would total in the hundreds of millions

of tons. [7] The assessed valuation of taxable property in 1895

---

5. Van Brunt, op. cit.

6. Ibid.

7. Franklin A. King, *caption to front cover drawing of steam
    engine at depot in Iron Junction, Missabe Iron Ranger, October
    1962

was $21,158. [8] Prospects were bright when rumors that the Duluth, Mesabi and Northern Railroad would build and expand the roundhouse, coal docks and section houses which contributed to most of the prosperity. However, the land for this project and a proposed

railroad yard, where headquarters would have to be located was to be purchased from one Stephen Ryan who, as it developed, would not agree to the reported offer of £18,000. [9]

ENGINE NO. 2, IRON JUNCTION DEPOT, 1893

The railroad moved its entire project to Proctor leaving no future for the budding city. Iron Junction declined rapidly when the decision to move was made, in 1895. Stores, saloons, hotels and homes were abandoned or moved. Only skeleton crews and families remained. Hotel Missabe remained in business for a few years after the exodus until the roundhouse was removed and the remaining tenants left. The depot then became the only remaining original building in Iron Junction. A pioneer couple, Mr. and Mrs. Emanuel Moline continued their grocery store along with a post office until Mr. Moline's death in 1957. Mrs. Moline maintained the business until 1961 when need for the utility ceased to exist.

---

8. Van Brunt, op. cit.

9. Zacher, William, op. cit.

(l-r) Moline Groc. & P. O., M. R. Johnson
Store, Ansley Saloon

INTERIOR OF MOLINE GROC., 1919

Stories of Iron Junction and its history exist in the memories

of its contemporaries. One of these was Etta Young, an eighteen

year old teacher at Shaw, who walked the three mile distance from

her school to Iron Junction's Downey Hotel where she lived, relates:

> ...When I first went to Iron Junction in 1897, many
> of the first settlers had already left, but there still
> remained a few who never tired of talking about the
> days of the thirteen saloons and four hotels and how
> their hopes for a little city were crushed when the
> railroad moved its shops to Proctorknott, as Proctor

was called in those days. They were inclined to blame Steve Ryan for their disappointment, feeling he should have been willing to accept the offer the railroad made for his property. [10]

In 1897, the Charles Zacher family moved to Iron Junction from Hibbing after their home and possessions were burned. [11] Mr. Zacher was given a job as section foreman and was the third to hold that job in the community. The Zacher family of four quite soon added the first birth recorded in Iron Junction when a girl was born to them in September, 1897. [12] Their arrival in "Iron" was welcomed by the Griersons, Ryans, McKaiges, Fitzpatricks, Ansleys, Dougals and several other families. [13]

Iron Junction was a service center. The many logging camps in the area were supplied with food, grain, feed for horses and other necessities all of which were shipped by train and stored in a warehouse behind the Ansley Saloon. In 1915, the Molines, who had purchased the original Klingensmith Grocery and Post Office, built another warehouse to store the feed and small farm equipment needed by the area people.

Iron Junction was also a fueling and watering station and for this purpose a large coal dock was built to hold nine or ten coal cars. Water for the engines was drawn from Elbow Creek by a steam

---

10. Young, Mrs. Etta, op. cit.

11. Woods, Mrs. Grace Zacher, resident of Iron Junction from 1897-1923, interview of August 4, 1964

12. Ibid.

13. Ibid.

operated McIntosh pumper. The storage tank which held the water was near the depot and remained there until 1905 when a new larger tank was placed across the street from the Moline store. At that time the first gasoline pump in the area was put into use to service the larger tank. From the very beginning, the tank leaked. In winter, a twenty foot icicle would form: in summer, drunks were placed beneath it to sober them up. [14] Shortly after its installation, the service foreman was killed by the new pump while inspecting it in motion. [15]

The volunteer fire department also used this water for their fire fighting purposes. Members of this necessary service were: William Zacher, Dan Perry, Tom Woods, Ole Christensen, Julius Nelson, and Dave Shoven. These men practiced regularly and were said to be quite

(l-r) Dan Perry, Tom Woods, Ole Christensen, William Zacher, Julius Nelson, Dave Shoven

efficient. [16]

School District number 25 was located just east of the Lowney

---

14. Zacher, Mr. William, op. cit.

15. Ibid.

16. Ibid.

Hotel. The one room building had a steeple, so typical of school houses in those days, and a bell which was rung in the morning, at noon and after school. Since there was no plumbing, the fa-

COUNTY SCHOOL NO. 25, IRON JUNCTION

INTERIOR, IRON JUNCTION SCHOOL

cilities were "out back." Children were given the task of keeping the fire burning during the school day so the room would be warm when school started. The first teacher in Iron Junction was Bridgett Godfrey followed by Mattie Lee, Agnes R. Holt, Marian K. Bain, Catherine McCurdy, Louise G. Lyons, and Lillian B. Gormley.[17]

Entertainment in this railroad town was simple according to Mrs. Etta Young, who was an early resident:

> ...Our life, as well as that of many others who lived in Iron, revolved around the activity and fortunes of the railroad. From early spring to late fall the ore trains rumbled through town. Six times a day there was a passenger train on the main line. The early morning hours were filled with the noise of freight trains loading and unloading....In summer, a circus train offered some variety....All the kids gathered to watch and wish they could have seen more.
>
> Social life in the early days was pretty much home-made. There were frequent dances held in the hotel and they were gay and lively enough to bring handcar loads from Eveleth, and they stayed and danced until dawn.
>
> The Christmas program at school constituted the extent of the theater, with the exception of David and Alice, a colored couple, billed as the one and only "White Face Comedians." Perhaps they failed to entertain the more sophisticated adults, but for days following their appearance, the children in town "played show."
>
> I recall one rather unusual evening which had us all entertained. A man, whose name I have long forgotten, drove a team of moose harnessed to a sleigh around town. He had trained the animals himself and later went on tour with them.
>
> There was always the woods, lakes and streams to turn to for hunting and fishing. I remember in hunting season, the frozen carcasses of deer piled high like cordwood on baggage trucks on the platform of the depot.
>
> Enough fish to fill a couple of wash tubs were often taken from Elbow Lake. This was before the lake was polluted by sewerage from Eveleth. It took the loss of fish and ducks plus years of effort and money to rectify this thoughtless contamination.
>
> Berry picking was an annual affair starting with wild strawberries, then on to raspberries, blueberries, pin cherries and high bush cranberries. Berry picking was an all day picnic which meant not only fun, but spending money for the younger generation....[18]

---

17. Woods, Mrs. Grace Zacher, op. cit.

18. Young, Mrs. Etta, op. cit.

Elbow Creek, which furnished water for the storage tanks, was

ELBOW LAKE AND EXCURSION BOAT, 1897

also a favorite swimming hole for the children. They delighted in having cool clear water running through their hometown, where a small dam just a short

distance north of the school created a much beloved pond, perfect for a refreshing dip. Elbow Lake itself had an excursion boat and for several of the earliest years families could go boating on a Sunday afternoon. [19] In the winter, when a blanket of snow covered the land and lakes had frozen over, children and adults donned their skates and the old swimming hole became an ice rink. The railroad later flooded a rink for skating. [20]

Mrs. Grace Zacher Woods describes additional activities of the young folks:

"...A Sunday night must was for the young people from small towns along the line to meet evening trains.

_____

19. "The Virginia Story", Historical Booklet of the Virginia Centennial Celebration, Virginia Chamber of Commerce, July 14, 1949

20. Young, Mrs. Etta, op. cit.

They would just stand on the platform and watch it
stop and go again. When it pulled away, the young
people usually went to one of the homes, spent the
evening singing and playing the piano. My mother had
a three gallon ice cream freezer full of ice cream
for us when it was our turn."[21]

A resident since 1912, Carl Lowry, now of Minneapolis, Minn-

esota, talks of early boyhood memories:

...The baseball field was a short distance west of
the Grierson's house and there was keen rivalry between Forbes and "Iron" on those Sunday games. Transportation was mostly by hand car. George Grierson and
I were bat and water boys.
    There was an Indian and His family named Wahboose
in the earlier days that lived about a mile east of
"Iron" towards Elbow Lake. He had a long trapline and
sold furs. He taught Merle Zacher the rudiments of
trapping and Merle in turn showed George and me the
Indian's secrets of trapping know how. [22]

These were busy but happy people. Everyone had a few chickens,

a cow and a vegetable garden, and canning was as regular as breath-

ing. Mrs. Zacher thought nothing of having to feed a whole engine

crew on just a moment's notice. [23] Young boys in the town were

given the task of keeping the four foot wide wooden sidewalk which

formed a rectangle around the entire business area, free of snow.

Mr. Zacher recalls one of the many amusing stories of early

railroading days:

"On a warm summer afternoon, a train stopped for refueling of coal and water. The brakeman got off with two
water jugs to be filled with cold water from the town
well which was located in the back room of the Ansley

---

21. Woods, Mrs. Grace Zacher, op. cit.

22. Lowry, Mr. Carl, resident of Iron Junction from 1900-1932, letter dated April 26, 1965

23. Woods, Mrs. Grace Zacher, op. cit.

Saloon. One he filled with water and the other with beer. As he emerged from the building, he was stopped by the superintendent and, was asked of the contents of the jugs.

"Water," was the reply by the nervous brakeman.

"Let me taste the water from one of your jugs."

Thoughtfully, he gave the superintendent one of the jugs to sample.

"Oh no, I want a taste of the other," demanded the superintendent.

The brakeman complied.

Cool, fresh water was what he received in this tasting. "All right, you may go." said the superintendent as he wiped his chin.

The brakeman walked quickly to the engine, relieved that he had made the correct decision by offering the jug with beer originally, hoping the superintendent would demand a taste of the other....[24]

Religion was an important aspect of life for the people of the junction city. Mrs. Grace Zacher Woods, reminising:

...We never had a church building at Iron Junction, but we had church services quite regularly. Missionaries and pastors from different denominations served us. When a minister came to town, in the early days, for an evening service, my mother served him supper, night's lodging and breakfast. I remember Reverend Langtry from Kelsey, Minnesota best. Reverend Lloyd Hunter and Reverend Burt Stanaway were both from Virginia. Reverend Stanaway organized the Sunday school, but there had been Sunday school for the children before that with different mothers having classes. In the winter, the pastors went to the homes or schoolhouse. These services stopped somewhere along about 1919 or so. Mrs. Moline, Mrs. Molander and Jessye Grierson were teachers for years. But, there was help from others. For years some residents of "Iron" were members of churches of their own choice in Eveleth, Virginia and Forbes. The train service at that time was very convenient....[25]

In spite of a rapid decline in its original population, Iron Junction remained a busy railroad center. Two passenger trains

---

24. Zacher, Mr. William, op. cit.

25. Woods, Mrs. Grace Zacher, op. cit.

ran daily from Virginia, Hibbing and Eveleth, to Duluth and return. For several years a passenger service called the "Flyer"
was offered, making it convenient for several students attend-
ing high school in Virginia.[26]

Medical facilities in Iron Junction in those days were at
a very minimum. Mrs. Etta Young tells of how the townspeople
remedied this situation:

> ...As the automobile is today, so was the hand car to
> the people of Iron Junction at this time. It was kept
> in the care of the section foreman and at any time, day
> or night, winter or summer, Mr. Zacher and a couple of
> his men might be called upon either to take someone to
> the doctor in Eveleth or to go after one for someone in
> "Iron". Quite often the stork arrived before the doc-
> tor, but in that case he usually found everything under
> control with a willing neighbor on hand. [27]

In 1919, the assessed valuation of Iron Junction was $1,575;
the population was ninety-two.[28] The railroad could do nothing
to bolster the economy of the town, and logging had slowed considerably. Slowly, the younger people were leaving, with the
older citizens remaining.

The successor to Merritt's D. M. & N. Railway, the Duluth Missabe and Iron Range Railway, had realized, as did the original
railroad, the strategic importance of "Iron" as a railroad center
and, as Mr. E. W. Anderson, General Superintendent of the Duluth
Missabe and Iron Range Railway states:

---

26. Woods, Mrs. Grace Zacher, op. cit.

27. Young, Mrs. Etta, op. cit.

28. Van Brunt, op. cit.

...The D.M. & N. Ry. began its service in 1892 with operations headquarters at Iron Junction, and this year, 1962, with the completion of a long range study, the Duluth Missabe and Iron Range Railway will come full circle. Once again operations headquarters for the Northern portion of the railroad will be located at Iron Junction.[29]

The center's value is expressed by Mr. J. G. Waits, Assistant Chief Engineer:

...The central location of the Operations Center to any present or possible future mining operations better prepares the railroad to meet transportation requirements, regardless of what district needs to be serviced. With an eye toward any mining area which may become prominent in the coming years and the physical layout of the railroad, the Iron Junction location of the Operations Center will be able to handle any volume of traffic in any direction. [30]

Some residents might be as reluctant as one former citizen in admitting to Iron Junction's being a ghost town. She prefers to think of it as a senior citizen--resting. [31]

29. Anderson, Mr. E. W., General Superintendent, "Reorganization of the Transportation Department, "Missabe Iron Ranger",October 1962

30. Waits, Mr. J. G., Assistant Chief Engineer, "Operation Center Construction," Missabe Iron Ranger, October 1962

31. Young, Mrs. Etta, op. cit.

-III-

CARSON LAKE, AN EARLY MINING LOCATION ON THE WEST MESABI

CARSON LAKE
ABOUT
1915-20

KEY TO MAP OF CARSON LAKE

1. Hamre Store (Old Hamre store that burned down in 1921)

2. Hamre Hardware and Post Office

3. Hamre Store (New store and tavern)

4. Murphy store and Pool Hall

5. Suzek residence

6. Raukar residence

7. Pintar residence

8. Poonich residence

9. Capan residence

10. Kolar residence

11. Pulis residence

12. Radinovich residence

13. Shane residence

14. Showhouse

15. Turkovich residence

16. Vojnovich residence

17. Pechina residence

18. Vzelac residence

19. Cavanaugh residence

20. Bosarich residence

21. Shafer residence

22. Opacich Residence

23. Madunich residence

24. Biondich residence

25. Milanovich residence

26. Malinar residence

KEY TO MAP OF CARSON LAKE (Continued)

27. Skrbich residence

28. Bigo residence

29. Novakovich residence

30. Milinovich residence

31. Worden residence

32. Horn residence

33. Patterson residence

34. Kelly residence

35. Bubalo residence

36. Unkovich residence

37. Clusica residence

38. Myer residence

39. Davidovich residence

40. Vladetich residence

41. Bjellos residence

42. Vukmir residence

43. Krompotich residence

44. Senich residence

45. Swikkinen residence

46. Javanovich residence

47. T. Davidovich residence

48. Carson Lake Bakery

49. Chanak residence

50. Sapon residence

51. Tomich residence

52. Perpich residence

KEY TO MAP OF CARSON LAKE (Continued)

53. Favero residence

54. Ongaro residence

55. Carpenter residence

56. Kelly residence

57. Gloomich residence

58. Kovich residence

59. Zbacnik residence

60. Cicimil residence

61. T. Shipka residence

CARSON LAKE

Six miles west of Hibbing, between the Carson Lake and Leetonia mines, mushroomed the Location of Carson Lake, which was
populated principally by Finns, Slovenians and Italians who
migrated across the Atlantic in search of a better life for
themselves and their families. The promise of a brighter future
in the mining country of Minnesota lured others from the Michigan
mines and from Canada.

THIS WAS THE REAL CARSON LAKE, 1903

The streets in
the location were
narrow and crooked
with deep ruts:
boulders and tree
stumps were plenti-
ful. In 1900, sev-
eral small tarpaper
miners' shacks were

scattered throughout the Location and were described by Mr. George

Chanak:

> ...Approximately five-hundred square feet is the area
> of this tarpaper home. In the kitchen is a wood stove,
> some firewood, and a barrel of water in one corner.
> Empty wooden dynamite boxes, piled one on top of the
> other, serve as cupboards. The tables and benches are
> homemade, with very few pieces of store bought furni-
> ture. The other rooms are also very small. The floor-
> ing is plain boards from wall to wall. As many as six
> to eight children sleep on two large beds in one room.
> A trap door on the floor takes you down into the cellar.
> Simplicity and ruggedness were, indeed, the cradle of

life for many....[1]

In 1910, the Leetonia and Morton underground mines employed about two hundred fifty men and when Carson Lake was drained in 1915, it offered another digging. [2] The call went out for more men to labor in the forthcoming mines. Soon the Carson Lake and other mines were producing ore. More people came to the area settling around the operations, the largest settlement developing at Carson Lake. The women converted the mining shacks into comfortable and attractive homes which were fenced in to corral the cows, pigs and chickens and, as families grew, homes were enlarged to meet their needs.

The land being developed for the rapidly growing Carson Lake Location was owned by the Great Northern Ore Properties of Hibbing which merely leased to the miners. Each built to suit his needs and his pocketbook although the Jones and Laughlin Mining Company built fifteen homes, some of which were used by mining officials.

To say the least, Carson Lake in the early 1900's epitomized a "rip-roaring" wild west town with robberies, shooting and nightly fights. [3] One witness told of two men fighting in front of the Tom Hamre Saloon only to stop momentarily while a lady and her

---

1. Chanak, George, "Farewell to Poverty and Happiness", an upublished pamphlet written of the days of Carson Lake Location, Hibbing, Minnesota, n. d.

2. Raukar, George, resident of Carson Lake from 1914-1951, interview of August, 1965

3. Ibid.

child walked by. But, as soon as they were out of earshot, they were right back at it. [4]

The first paycheck for almost every miner was partially used to buy a knife or a gun. A trip was made into Hibbing where the Montgomery Ward catalog was the usual source of supply. It is said that few miners were without their weapons at any time after work hours. [5] During the weekly poker game at the Hamre Saloon, it was not unusual to see a revolver or knife along side of one's money. [6] In the "big games" where as much as $800 could be seen on the table, it was not unlikely that you would find such card sharks or "slikkers" from Hibbing as "Pipeline Jack", and "Two Fingered Bob." [7] These men were said to have made their living on the winnings at Carson Lake. [8] It is no wonder that this location of hard working, hard drinking and hard fighting men gained the reputation of a "battle ground." [9]

The men were making "big" money. Those who were skilled, brave enough and healthy, worked in the underground mines. It was customary to work underground under a contract which established the rate to be paid for each one-ton ore car coming out of

---

4. Raukar, op. cit.

5. Ibid.

6. Ibid.

7. Ibid.

8. Ibid.

9. Ibid.

the shaft, fifty to eighty-five cents being an average rate. The miners, however, had to pay for the dynamite they used to get that same ore out. Needless to say, the men put a lot more back into their digging to avoid having to use any more dynamite than they had to. Because of the extreme dangers and poor working conditions, underground miners were paid slightly more than those in the open pits. They were, however, proud to be underground miners and, compared to the open pit miners, considered themselves craftsmen in their field. Because of this attitude, there was constant competition between the mines. The majority of underground miners were immigrants. [10] They worked in pairs and were usually of the same nationality. Finns were noted for their ability to crib in difficult shafts. [11] The work was extremely hazardous and the mortality rate high, justifying their pay of eight to ten dollars as compared to two dollars a day for others. [12] The Morton mine was sunk in quicksand and took several lives. [13]

Many of the immigrants would quite often bring homemade bread, canned goods, and the like, to the mine captains hoping to insure their job tenure. Mr. Raukar, during our interview, related:

> "...A yellow slip given to a man meant his services were no longer needed. Frequently, the mining captain would come to work with several of these yellow slips clearly exposed for the men to see. Each man, of course, imagined one of the slips would be his walking papers; so,

---

10. Raukar, op. cit.

11. Ibid.

12. Ibid.

13. Ibid.

he broke his back all day hoping to impress the captain
and possibly encourage him to reconsider letting him go.
More often than not, there were no names on th yellow
slips." [14]

The superintendent of the Carson Lake underground and open pit
mines from the years 1905-1932 was Everett S. Tillinghast. Mr.
Tillinghast is well remembered because of the influence he had
upon the people of Carson Lake. Born in East Hampton, Long Island,
he settled in Hibbing in 1905 as a member of the Interstate Mining
Company and during his long life enjoyed respect and admiration
as "Mr. T" by every man who had any association with him. [15] In
a tribute to him in the Engineering and Mining Journal for which he
had written monthly articles, a Jones and Laughlin official described him:

> ...I have yet to hear any one of his old employees
> who had anything but good to say about him.... [16]

Only upon his death did many people learn of his work with
foundling boys, and for CARE, the program of self help for poverty stricken peoples. [17] One old acquaintance tells of the day he
and some other youngsters took a broken cart wheel to the mine
blacksmith:

> ...coming to the mine, we sensed it was not operating.
> They had had a major breakdown. We entered the black-

---

14. Raukar, op. cit.

15. Lawrence, Saunder, resident of Carson Lake Location from 1910-
     1947, interview of July, 1965

16. "A Tribute to Mr. E.S. Tillinghast," Engineering and Mining
     Journal, written by a Jones and Laughlin official, n.d.

17. Raukar, op. cit.

smith shop, and the world stopped. Standing opposite us was Mr. Tillinghast and two of his top men. He came over, looked at the wheel, and said, "Well, well, boys, you have trouble too." He gave the wheel to the black- smith and said,"When you get time, fix it. The boys expect a good job. Otherwise they will have to come back.... [18]

Mr. Tillinghast's home was protected during Halloween by the children themselves from the vandals' work. Mrs. Tillinghast would often invite a few of the children of Carson Lake, Harold and Leetonia Locations in for cookies and milk. It was indeed a thrill to be invited to play tennis on their clay courts. Phil- anthropic deeds for employees were kept a secret from Eastern officials. [19] From Carson Lake and the Agnew mines, "Mr. T" moved to Virginia, Minnesota as Superintendent of the Lincoln mine and from there to Calumet. He retired in 1946 after serving with the Jones and Laughlin Mining Company for twenty-six years. He died in 1962 at the age of eighty-three.

In those early days, the family was a closely knit group with each member contributing to its survival. Each was respon- sible for his share of the household chores. The two big chores for the men and boys of the family were the planting and cultiv- ating of a garden, and the gathering and chopping of firewood. Among their daily chores were the necessary tasks of cleaning the barn, and hauling water. And, then there were the seasonal chores of haying, picking berries, shoveling snow and mending fences. [20]

---

18. "A Tribute to Mr. E.S. Tillinghast", op. cit.

19. Raukar, op. cit.

20. Ibid.

The young girl's contributions also varied. Families were large and often there were boarders. Consequently, the young women helped their mothers in every way they could. Along with scrubbing, cooking, washing by hand, the daughters helped with the livestock. After the harvest in the fall, the job of canning began, with the women preparing hundreds of jars of food to carry the family through the winter. Then, just before winter, the butchering season began with the cutting of meat, making sausages and smoking the meat.

Even with so much work to do, the Location children found time for self-made entertainment:

...In the springtime...the swollen creeks were targets. to be followed by large marble playing contests and the building of bird houses and chipmunk traps.
    In the summertime, building a camp was a big challenge. Broken boards, used tin, nails, tar paper, and managable trees comprised the inventory. To keep the whereabouts of the camp a secret was accomplished by camouflage and diversion....Those wonderful days would take us over many paths, trails, and abandoned logging roads, leading us to everywhere and nowhere. To climb to the top of the dumps, or mountains, if you please, was both dangerous and exciting....Other pleasures included the building of a raft with ties or poles and navigating it in the pond and occasionally taking a spill along with your dog....There was an abandoned pit we called the canyon, and there the good swimmers went....Farther beyond were several small lakes and the opportunity to watch the beavers....to go on the raft... launch a homemade boat. It sank in a few minutes!...
    As for fun in the location, there were so many games to play, with the sheds and haystacks making good hiding places. Carving whistles from branches, toy carpentry, jackknife exhibitions, and the lying on the ground and gazing at the sky and clouds were additional gems of fun....the steam shovels....the dumping of the one ton wooden ore cars...the miners and their carbide lamps or candles...the blacksmith shop...the ever so dangerous open pit mines...the chugging dinky, with its small train or ore cars, was simply cute! Once in awhile the dinky's engineer would give us a treat by spinning the wheels,

faking a power loss....This is about the place to talk
about naughty boys. The push car, the hand car, and
the scooter left on a side track over the week-end
are clues enough, and then let your imagination go to
work! [21]

School w s important to the Location's residents, espec-
ially in the family where the parents had had no formal school-
ing. In many of the homes most of the speaking was done in a
non-English language. Thus, there were always the few at school
who took pleasure in mimmicking the accents of the youngsters
from these homes. The problem was usually solved with an in-
vitation to take a walk over the hill after school.

Mr. Chanak remembers:

...Kindergarten was fun. Playing with toys we had
never seen was only part of it. Our school was very
neat. For the first time many of us walked on var-
nished hardwood floors. The school had running water,
and turning on the faucet was amazing to us. Indoor
washroom facilities seemed mysterious. The school had
electricity, and was that ever something! And, add to
that the telephone!...School was the opening of a new
world.... [22]

Two of the earliest teachers in Carson Lake were a Miss Sa-
therwaite, who was remembered as being a kindly lady who often
shared cookies with the children, and the teacher-principal,
Mr. Roy Martin. [23] The janitor for many years was a Mr. Olson
who made the children wipe their feet when they entered the
building. A moderate apartment on the second story was occupied continually by some of the teachers who taught in the

---

21. Chanak, op. cit.

22. Ibid.
23. Raukar, op. cit.

building. Later on, as travel became less of a chore, most of the teachers preferred to live in Hibbing and commute to the Location each day. The new teachers in the Hibbing system usually taught in the location schools while those with a few years experience frequently went back to civilization. [24]

The miners, out of necessity, made frequent trips into Hibbing for hardware supplies and mining equipment. An enterprising young man by the name of Tom Hamre investigated the possibility of opening a hardware and mining equipment store in the location. After clearing through legal channels, in 1916, Mr. Hamre opened his place of business much to the satisfaction of the miners and their families. The store soon added a grocery and meat section and in a few short years, the store employed ten clerks. Groceries were delivered to the homes in a horse-drawn wagon in the summer and sleigh in the winter. A short time later, Mr.

HAMRE STORE AND POST OFFICE

Hamre was granted permission by the Great Northern Ore Properties to erect a building to house a saloon and an addition to the hard-

_____

24. Raukar, op. cit.

ware store to set up a post office.

A luxury enjoyed by few, if any, other locations was the erection of a showhouse, again by the skilled business hand of Mr. Hamre. Silent films were brought into the Location and shown twice a week. The children were charged ten cents and watched wide-eyed as Hoot Gibson skillfully played the piano to set the mood. For some of the younger generation, it became customary to go down across from the saloon after the Saturday evening show to watch the fights. [25] Occasionally they would be scared off by the flash of a switchblade or the appearance of a pistol. [26]

The front porch of the Hamre Saloon was the central meeting place of the Location and it was on this porch that many of the problems of the world were solved. Those who were literate would tell others what they had read, coloring the news with their own viewpoint. [27] On occasion they would read an article directly out of the newspaper. These men were looked up to and respected. [28]

In 1908 a hospital was set up in a Company house, adding an important service to the community. [29] Mr. Hamre added another business to his enterprises in 1917 by turning an aban-

25. Raukar, op. cit.

26. Ibid.

27. Ibid.

28. Ibid.

29. Michelson, H. O., resident of Carson Lake Location from 1901-1950, interview of July, 1965

doned building into a lunch counter and hired a young couple to
run it. By this time the Location's businesses included a hard-
ware-grocery and meats store, a post office, a show house, saloon,
and a bakery most of which were run by Mr. Hamre. [30] Not until
1921 did the final place of business appear: Mr. Paul Heffer-
man opened a pool hall. The men of the Location were soon spend-
ing much of their free time perfecting their game. But, it wasn't
long before the younger generation made their appearance as often
as they were permitted and soon became superior players. [31]

In 1916 a horse drawn "bus line" was initiated by Mr. Hamre
and Paul Morris to service the 2,000 residents of Carson Lake
and the residents of Leetonia, Utika, Morton, Kerr, and Harold
Locations. The horse drawn bus with seats all facing the outside,
accommodated seventeen passengers. A vain attempt was made to
enclose the passenger section during the winter but it was said
that it was colder inside than out. [32] Needless to say, few
used the horse drawn sleigh during the blustery winter months.
Mr. Charles Shubat of Hibbing later took over the busline and
introduced a motorized automobile, the Model T. [33] The ride actually became enjoyable. [34] This service continued by Mr. Shubat

---

30. Michelson, op. cit.

31. Raukar, op. cit.

32. Ibid.

33. Shubat, Charles, owner of the Northern Transportation Company,
    interview of August, 1965, Hibbing, Minnesota

34. Raukar, op. cit.

until 1950 when the automobile population increased and it became financially impossible to continue the run. [35]

Tragedy struck Carson Lake on November 10, 1917, just a month
after the Moose Lake fire. Two boys playing with matches in an
old abandoned building started a fire which burned a total of
forty-four buildings including the showhouse, a horse barn, the
doctor's office, Hamre Hardware Grocery and Meats, and forty
homes. [36] The flames, excited by forty mile per hour winds,
moved quickly through the tarpaper shacks. The mines closed
down and the men were released to save their homes or salvage
what they could. Word was relayed to the **Hibbing Fire Depart-**
ment as quickly as was possible in 1917, but the fires were
raging when the two small units arrived. Carsonites worked fe-
verishly with poor equipment including buckets, water soaked
sacks and a couple of small pumps, all of which proved to be
quite useless. Those families, whose homes were not in immedi-
ate danger, helped to remove the belongings from the homes already hot from the quickly spreading fires. Hibbing's fire units
could do little with their water capacity of 500 gallons. Just
as progress was being made, the two units had to return to the
public water taps for refills. The inferno was stopped only by
dynamite experts who, after having several homes evacuated and
emptied of all the contents, blew up the structures. It was a

---

35. Shubat, op. cit.

36. Milinovich, Joe, resident of Carson Lake Location from 1915-
    1940, letter dated May 15, 1962

miracle that more homes were not lost. The clean-up task was a sorrowful one, in spite of neighborly help to rebuild.

Mr. Chanak relates several lurid incidents in the mining location:

> ...As for the black sheep, we had our share of them...
> Being a new mining camp, there were the fights, gambl-
> ing and drinking, especially among the single men. One
> evening,"the bull of the Location" was strutting around
> with a chip on his shoulder, daring anyone to knock it
> off. Here is how one fellow did it. First he emptied
> his six-gun into the bull and very simply the chip took
> care of itself. On another occasion, a gal played a fellow
> for Santa Claus. When he got wise, he played two-way
> Russian roulette with all the chambers fully loaded....Just
> before suppertime we were playing, and suddenly a blast in
> the house next door blew part of the roof sky high! Mama
> said that it was an accident - probably a left-over piece
> of dynamite embedded in mining timber used for firewood.
> Years later, an eager tongue told us a different version
> and insisted that it wasn't an accident. It was alleged
> that the husband was suspicious about his wife and the
> star boarder and that it was simply a matter of attempt-
> ed liquidation. Incidentally, at the time for the explo-
> sion, the wife and the boarder were doing chores and con-
> sequently escaped injury. 37

Prohibition had extreme effect on the people of Carson Lake, as it did with most people of our country, and what a field for stories! Moonshiners, bootleggers, federal agents and blind pigs contributed to the jargon. 38 Hibbing, being in Indian Territory, was dry, and the closest town where the alcoholic beverages could be purchased was Buhl. The back trails from Buhl to the Hibbing area were well traveled by anything and everything that could carry a bottle of whatever alcoholic beverages that could be

---

37. Chanak, op. cit.

38. Ibid.

bought. [39] These bootleggers would sometimes be followed by
those who watched to see where the "beverages" would be sup-
posedly well-hidden. When the time was right, they'd take all
they could manage to get away with. Concealment was mostly in
the back woods, in a haystack, or, during crisis, even in a man-
ure pile! [40]

One citizen, who wishes to remain anonymous, told of a story
which took place during the prohibition:

> ...Dad brought home a bottle in his lunch bucket, and
> no sooner get it out and onto the table when a "fed"
> was seen coming up the walk. Mom and dad already con-
> ceded the fact that they'd been caught and the punish-
> ment of a fine or jail sentence was inevitable. I was
> only twelve, continued the former Carson Lake citizen,
> but I grabbed the bottle and dropped it into the water
> barrel next to the table just as the agent stepped into
> the doorway. "I froze." The agent made a brief search
> of the kitchen and, seemingly satisfied, started to
> leave. He passed me, and asked if I was fetching water.
> I nodded yes as he walked out the door...."

Some were not so fortunate. Every week moonshine stills
were found in the Location or in the woods and federal agents
broke up the operations which were only rebuilt elsewhere.
Though the residents knew the federal agents had a job to do,
they resented their visits.

Before 1905, Hibbing used Carson Lake for its water supply,
and horse drawn wagons with wooden barrels were used to haul the
water to its residents. Not until 1914 did Carson Lake receive
running water, of a sort. A one-inch pipe was laid from the

39. Raukar, op. cit.

40. Ibid.

Leetonia mine where a pump had been set up and from the faucet
to which it led, 1,500 people drew water for a number of years.
As many as thirty to forty people would often stand in line for
their turn at the faucet. It was usually the boys' jobs to
bring barrels in a wagon to be filled for home use.

As the size of the mines increased, the prospect of moving the Location became evident and in the 1950's Carson Lake
like other communities of its kind, met that fate. Residents
were offered a residential lot in Kelly Lake for as little as
$150. [41] Some families had their houses moved, while others
held until basements and a few other assessments were provided
for them. Finally, when they were given the ultimatum of having the W. S. Moore Company of Hibbing move them at Company expense, or pay for the moving themselves if they had not done so
within thirty days, the remaining families complied.

One former resident aptly describes the departure:

> ...Due to expanded mining operations and living on
> leased land, that dreaded time came when we had to
> move....On that day I happened to come home during
> the working day and found mama and her friend stand-
> ing on the road, both of them in solemn silence and
> on the verge of tears. For nearby soon they would
> be moving the house of another dear friend. The
> three of them had been close friends for many years.
> Soon the moving caravan went by us down the road
> and closely followed behind was their friend, rid-
> ing in a car with her son. As I was consoling Mama,
> her friend, who was standing near her, ran after the
> car for a short distance. And as she did so, she
> waved and sobbed, "GOOD-BYE! GOOD-BYE! GOOD-BYE! [42]

---

41. Raukar, op. cit.

42. Chanak, op. cit.

-IV-

EARLY MINING VILLAGES ON EAST MESABI

A. VILLAGE OF LEONIDAS (OLD LOCATION, NEW LOCATION AND "GROSS 40")

VILLAGE OF LEONIDAS

SET-UP TRACKS

AVE.

11
10
9
8
7
6
5
4
3
2

12
13
14
15
16
17
18
19
20
21

AVE.

37
36
35
34
33

SPRUCE HILL →

1

22
23
24
25
26

A

32
31
30
29
28

B

27

38

OLD
LOCATION
ABOUT 1911

47

GROSS 40
ABOUT 1915

4TH   ST.

3RD   ST

NEW
LOCATION
ABOUT 1916

46

2ND   ST.

D.S. & N. RY.

48

39

40

1ST   ST.

CNTY. RD. NO. 20

45

44

43

41
42

TO EVELETH →

WEST EVELETH ABOUT 1921

N ↑

KEY TO MAP OF VILLAGE OF LEONIDAS (Including - Old Location about 1911: New Location about 1916: Gross 40: and West Eveleth about 1921)

1. Residence of Mr. Willard Bayliss and family (Mr. Bayliss was the Assistant Superintendent for the Oliver Iron Mining Company)

2. Residence of Vic Ramponi

3. Sutton residence

4. Residence of Captain Benson

5. Residence of Steve Ramponi

6. Residence of Emil Laukka

7. Residence of Oscar Castren

8. Residence of Dick Eddy

9. Residence of Magnus Magnuson

10. Residence of Harold Mitchell

11. Residence of Ed Kane

12. Roach residence

13. Residence of Pete Lenossi

14. Residence of Ed Kissel

15. Bonjioni residence

16. Peters residence

17. Residence of Harry Laury

18. Residence of Matt Eikola

19. Anstess residence

20. Residence of Ernie St. Jean

21. Residence of Grant Rogers

22. Residence of Fred Granross

23. Residence of Bill Cox

KEY TO MAP OF VILLAGE OF LEONIDAS (continued)

24. Residence of Fred Williams

25. Residence of Jack Hill

26. Residence of John DeRosse

27. Village Hall

28. Barfknecht residence

29. Residence of Sanford Weerri

30. Residence of Charles Olson

31. Residence of John Hendrickson

32. Peterson Boarding House

33. Barfknecht residence

34. Residence of Emil Vandell

35. Stetzler residence

36. Houston residence

37. Holder residence

38. Company tennis courts and skating rink

39. First school (erected in 1910)

40. Second school with addition (erected in 1914, the addition being
    constructed in 1919)

41. Original Postudensek Grocery (in basement of residence)

42. Present Postudensek Grocery

43. Tousignant Grocery

44. Hammer Grocery and Post Office

45. Nemanich General Merchandise (Eveleth's old More Hospital build-
    ing)

46. New Location's park and playground

KEY TO MAP OF VILLAGE OF LEONIDAS (continued)

47. Pump house

48. Foot bridge over railroad tracks (constructed shortly after the development of the New Location to make it safer for the school children to cross the busy railroad tracks)

LEONIDAS

(Old Location, New Location, and Gross 40)

The Old Location of Leonidas had its beginning in 1909 when the Oliver Iron Mining Company moved its shops from the Adams Hill Location in Eveleth. Mining there was already in progress and explained the need for a community. A year later the town was born when the Grande Construction Company of Virginia built thirty-four homes and a boarding house to afford accomodations for the men. [1] Homes were erected hastily and application for them was on a "first-come first-serve" basis. Among the first residents were Mr. and Mrs. Fred Williams who, like many others, considered in making their selection the number of boulders found in the yard, as it was no easy task having them removed.[2] In a short time, all thirty-four homes and boarding house were occupied and the assistant superintendent, a Mr. Willard Bayliss, and his family had settled in their roomy residence which had been moved from Eveleth. As mining operations increased, additional men were employed, but for those workers not living in the Location, it was a three mile walk to Eveleth. By 1909, there were already 150 men underground. [3]

The Leonidas underground mining property was owned by the

---

1. Mr. Ed Mills, resident of Leonidas Location from 1911-1940, interview of July 1965

2. Ibid.

3. Ibid.

state and leased by the Oliver Iron Mining Company. Being there were no skips in the shafts, the wooden cars were raised and lowered by steam hoist, hand loaded underground and dumped by three men above. Not a pound of ore had been shipped from the Leonidas from 1908 to 1914 because it was being stockpiled for future use.[4]

Working in water above the ankles was quite common although pumps

 worked continually to keep the men in the shafts from drowning. Two ten inch pipes on the surface handled the water from underground and

EARLY STEAM ENGINE IN LEONIDAS SWITCH YARD

carried it to Three Mile Lake a short distance away.

In 1908, the Oliver Mining Company was working the Leonidas open pit which was small in diameter and very deep. Because of its similarity, the men called it the "Rat Hole".[5] Also, leased property of the Hull-Nelson mine was purchased by the Oliver Mining Company and excavations from the Leonidas were made connecting them.

Three hydrants were installed in the Old Location by 1912, and water was drawn from them for daily use. In the winter, the

----

4. Mill, Ed, op. cit.

5. Ibid.

hydrants would freeze and in order to get the water it was necessary to thaw them by pouring hot water over the top. Residents would watch from their window hoping one of the neighbors would thaw the hydrants before it was necessary for them to brave the cold to draw their water. [6]

The only sidewalks in the Location were those made by each family from the house to the street, but in 1913, a wooden walk was constructed extending from the "Old Location" to the schoolhouse corner and east to Spruce Hill which was the boundary of Eveleth. Mrs. Hulda Hammer tells about the walk from the Location to Eveleth:

> ...In those days the women didn't have the low, flat shoes we have now for walking. The women at that time wore high top shoes with high French heels and every time a woman went to town, she'd pull a heel off as there was a space between the boards in the sidewalk. Everyone had to have two pairs of dress shoes, wearing one pair and carrying the other to the shoemaker... [7]

Wooden sidewalks were replaced by concrete in 1919, and walks were also laid along each side of the street. Trees were provided by the mining company and all of the families in the Location planted one along the boulevards.

Residents of the Old Leonidas Location were "One Big Happy Family". [8] Most were willing to give his neighbor a helping hand. Ed Mills, one of Leonidas Location's oldest residents, gives an

---

6. Mills, Ed, op. cit.

7. Hammer, Mrs. Hulda, resident of Leonidas Location from 1915-1920, interview of August 1964

8. Mills, Ed, op. cit.

account of neighborliness:

> ...Ed Kane's house, which lay at the bottom of three
> small grades, in the spring of 1915 was flooded by
> water from melting snow. Several chickens drowned
> and, in the house there were six to eight inches of
> water. Several neighbors worked all afternoon rais-
> ing the piano to the ceiling with planks and blocks
> of wood to keep it dry....[9]

There were no sewers in the Location to handle water "run-

off", but, in 1915, the Mining Company appointed Richard Stephens

as foreman and several men to dig a three mile trench from the Lo-

cation t o Three Mile
Lake. The digging
took the men four
months, but this
trench was quite
adequate and is still
used today by the Vil-
lage of Leonidas.

"RUN-OFF" TRENCH

Company benefits and privileges were varied and many, among

these the purchase of coal which the Company sold to its workers. [10]

Hard coal cost $8.25 a ton as compared to $11.50 a ton in Eveleth

or in Virginia. Soft coal, although extremely dirty, was used more

frequently because of its low cost of $2.00 a ton. Wood was free,

but families were expected to haul it from the Company supply.

One form of recreation was provided with the building of tennis

9. Mills, Ed, op. cit.

10. Ibid.

courts across the main road from the Location. Racquets were a-vailable at the Mining Company's warehouse at cost. Repairs and maintenance of the courts were handled by Company workers and when the winter snow arrived, the tennis courts were flooded creating a large skating rink. At Christmas, colored lights were hung above the rink to add much to the holiday spirit. Christmas Eve day Santa could be seen riding on a mule-drawn sleigh, the beast furnished with deer antlers tied to its head. Waldron Hol-

der, the first Santa in the Location, would travel annual-ly to all of the chil-dren's homes to bring them candy. [11] Later, this delightful task was handled by Ed Mills. [12] Another special holiday cus-

SANTA (WALDRON HOLDER), MULE AND SLEIGH

tom was the annual night of caroling when Eveleth band members joined residents and their families in music and song.

Business life in Leonidas was virtually non-existent. There were no stores, but fortunately, the Peterson and Damberg Grocery stores were willing to deliver. Mail was usually brought in from

---

11. Mills, Ed, op. cit.

12. Ibid.

Eveleth by the Oliver Mining Company supply truck driven by Jake Random at the cost of twenty-five cents a month which was paid to him. [13] Others picked it up in Eveleth. The Location's centre of activity was the Carolyn Peterson Boarding House. Waldron Holder, whose audience would sit around the pot bellied stove, would read stories and give imitations to add to the enjoyment of the stories. [14]

"Gross 40", where ore had been stockpiled and later removed, was a berry patch. Raspberries, blueberries, strawberries and gooseberries were plentiful and berry picking was a "fruitful" endeavor for Leonidas residents.

The Company built an ice house in 1911 and Ed Kane, who was hired to deliver ice, chose the fortunate few who had it delivered twice a week and cut to fit each individual ice box. [15] This service continued until 1923 when the refrigerator became widely used and ice was no longer practical.

Leonidas lay on the southern boundary of Nichols Township, thus making it part of the Mountain Iron School District. In 1910, at the cost of $12,000, a two room frame structure was built housing grades one to eight. [16] The first teachers were a Miss Jensen, Miss Pfeiffer and a Mr. Stetzler who also assumed the

---

13. Mills, Ed, op. cit.

14. Peterson, Mr. Horton, resident of Leonidas Location from 1912-1940, interview of August 1965

15. Mills, Ed, op. cit.

16. Ibid.

role of principal and custodian. [17] In a few years, however, a

FIRST SCHOOL IN LEONIDAS

NEW BRICK STRUCTURE

fine, new brick structure was built to accomodate the increased

enrollment. But, it, too, soon became inadequate, and in 1919

an addition was made which included eight more classrooms, a

manual training section, domestic science department and a gym-

nasium. Upper grades were transported by Mountain Iron buses

to Eveleth until 1942 when the Village of Leonidas became part

_____

17. Mills, Ed, op. cit.

of the Eveleth School District. Eventually, in 1945, all of the children

were trans-

ported to Ev-

eleth and the

Leonidas

School was

closed, much

NEW SCHOOL WITH ADDITION (ORIG. SCH. IN BACKGROUND)

to the disappointment of the remaining residents. [18]

Sunday schools were organized as early as 1913 by Mr. Jack Hill. [19] There was no affiliation with any particular church and permission was given by the Mountain Iron Superintendent of Schools, Mr. Minch, to use the school for the classes if the responsibility would be taken by someone to keep the fire banked and hot water in the radiators. Mr. Mills, who was placed in charge of a group of non-conformists who chose not to attend Sunday school, agreed to take care of that job. His boys, who now took a keener interest in the class because of a male teacher, consisted of: Horton Peterson, Chelsey Williams, Frank Greenross, Robert Holder, Vic Ramponi, Waino Eikola, Robert Granross and Rolland Rogers. [20] To hold their interest, Mr. Mills introduced games, one of which was basketball, the equipment consisting of a ball and a wastepaper basket. Because of its non-affiliation, the Sunday school Christ-

18. Mills, Ed, op. cit.

19. Ibid.

20. Ibid.

mas programs were well attended. Money to buy Bibles and child-ren's books which were given to the graduates of the Sunday school classes was earned by the children who presented programs and put on ice cream socials. Oliver Mining Company employees would go out of their way to buy ice cream from the children. At Christ-mas the children bought a $10 basket of groceries for each of the two largest families in the Location.

In 1915, thirty homes were moved in by the Company from Old Messaba and Adams Hill to the area known as "Gross 40". [21] Old Leonidas residents referred to the new development as the New Location.

ORIGINAL TOWNSHIP HALL

Old Leonidas Location was in the Nichols Township with the town hall erected on the south side of the Location, and Township meetings were held there until 1917 when a more central location named Parkville became the site for a new town hall. The old building was purchased in its entirety by Leonidas to become the centre for social gatherings and meetings.

The leaders of Leonidas Location were quick to realize that

21. Mills, Ed, op. cit.

because of the high mineral valuation, as attempt would be made by

HALL AS IT STANDS TODAY

Eveleth officials to bring the Location into the city limits of Eveleth. [22] Probably this was the main reason why, on September 5, 1917, a petition signed by H. E. Mitchell, R. H. Stephens, W. J. Matters and twenty-nine other residents of Leonidas Location, was present- ed to the St. Louis County Com-

missioners, requesting incorporation as the Village of Leonidas, the whole embracing 880 acres, part of the acreage having been platted as "Leonidas" and part as "Gross". [23] The petition states that a census taken at the time showed that there were 275 persons living in the area for which corporate powers were asked. [24] On motion of Commissioner Pentilla, the petition was adopted on Sep- tember 7, 1917, with the election ordered for October 8, 1917 in the town hall. [25] At the election, forty-six unanimous votes were cast. [26] At the subsequent first election for officers, the fol-

---

22. Ed Mills, op. cit

23. Van Brunt, Walter, Duluth and St. Louis County Minnesota (Chic- ago and New York, 1921) Vol. II

24. Ibid.

25. Ibid.

26. Ibid.

lowing became the original council of the Village of Leonidas:
R. Trevarthen, President; E. J. Kane, W. J. Matters, and W. Holder,
Trustees: H. E. Mitchell, Clerk. [27]

The southern limit of the Village was County road number 20.
Across this road several homes had been built and had been given
the name of West Eveleth. Mr. Nemanich, a resident of Eveleth,
bought the old More Hospital, moved it to West Eveleth and stocked it with general merchandise which pleased the people of the Village. [28] Several other residents of West Eveleth opened establish-
ments. Mr. Postudensek stocked his basement and opened a grocery
store in 1921, and in the same year,
Mrs. Hammer and Joseph Tousignant
also opened grocery stores. Mrs.
Hammer, soon after opening, received
authority to open a post office in
her store. [29] A meeting was called
to decide on a name for the post
office and the general feeling was
that it should be Leonidas, but the
inspector, the late Mr. Fleming,
thought it unwise to have that name

HAMMER GROC. & P. O.

as there is also a Leonidas in Michigan. He felt sure there would

---

27. Van Brunt, op. cit.

28. Hammer, op. cit.

29. Ibid.

be much missent mail, so he proposed to draft a new name of Leoneth by taking "Leon" from Leonidas and "eth" from Eveleth. [30]

In 1923, the Oliver Mining Company built twenty-eight new homes in the New Location and these remain in the Village today. Unlike earlier Company houses, they had the conveniences of indoor plumbing. However, old homes moved in from Old Messaba and Adams Hill were given the same convenience by the addition of an extra room to the rear of the house.

Millions of tons of iron ore were moving south to the docks in Duluth, and the steam shovels worked around the clock to gouge the earth with buckets, the size of which grew larger each year. On the "Iron Range", cities often had to be moved to make way for these hungry earth movers. The Old Location of Leonidas was no exception. In 1941, the Oliver Mining Company homes were sold at a unit price of fifty dollars per room which was considered a fair price. [31] Some of the tenants bought their homes and moved them to foundations elsewhere on the Range while others bought theirs to sell for a profit.

Two years later, all of the homes in the New Location were sold, but since the Oliver Iron Mining Company felt that the expense of maintenance offered the tenants of the employees' homes was too great, they were sold in the same manner as at the Old Location. [32] Only the homes brought in from Old Messaba and

---

30. Hammer, op. cit.

31. Mills, Ed, op. cit.

32. Ibid.

Adams Hill to the area called "Cross 40" were removed, leaving the
twenty-two newer homes to make up the present Village of Leonidas.
And so, another mining village all but disappeared and only a few
of the old families remain to recount their memories of the "good
old days".

B.   VILLAGE OF SPINA

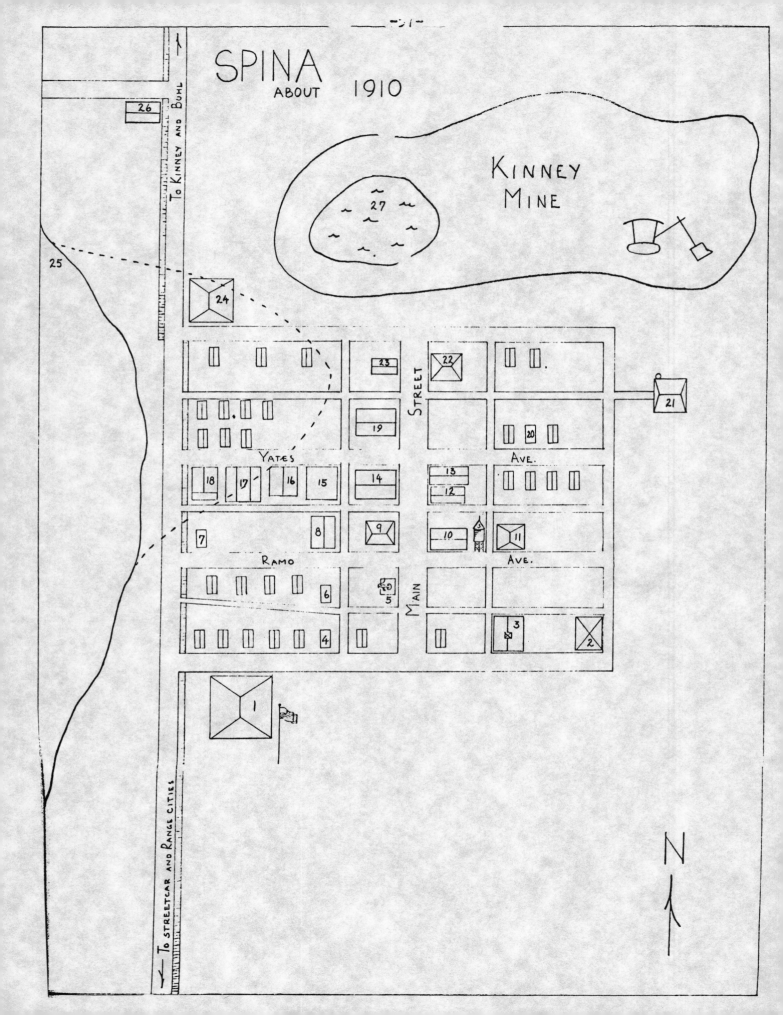

SPINA
ABOUT 1910

KINNEY MINE

KEY TO MAP OF SPINA

1. Hartley School

2. Pump House

3. Original school (presently a residence in Buhl)

4. Residence of Mr. Joe Squillace and his wife

5. Town pump

6. Empty weather-beaten house (formerly Belfiori residence)

7. Empty house (building still standing)

8. Town bakery

9. Empty confectionery store

10. Saloon

11. Village Hall and Fire Department

12. Bank

13. Saloon

14. Cordileone Saloon and Grocery

15. Empty Saloon

16. Clothing store

17. Jarvi Dairy Store

18. Clothing store

19. Medure Grocery

20. Tuck residence (home still standing but owners, Mr. and Mrs. Tuck, are in rest homes in Virginia and Biwabik respectively)

21. Power house

22. Finnish sauna

23. Barber shop

24. Johnson Boarding House

KEY TO MAP OF SPINA (continued)

25. Dean Mine Dump (dotted line indicates extent of slide)

26. McCoy Saloon

27. Spina's water supply

SPINA

Sometime in 1896, Spina had its beginning as a real estate venture with a purchase of land by two bachelors named Peter and Pasqual Spina. The parcel of land was located near the Dean, Kinney, Yates, Seville and several other mines which made it a convenient location for the men to be able to walk to work. Huge timber covered the entire area making it necessary for the land to be logged before small tarpaper shacks could be temporarily erected. By 1901, however, more permanent buildings had been built.

SPINA, 1920, FROM DEAN MINE DUMP

One would need to look very closely to find evidences that Spina ever existed. Its name is quite unfamiliar to most people of the Mesabi Range today. In 1913, however, it was a quiet mining village of two hundred or more people. Now all that remains of what was once Spina are two families, the Tucks and the Joe Squillaces, both early settlers. On a warm summer afternoon, Mr. and Mrs. Joe Squillace shared cold watermelon with my family and, with a keen memory, pointed out where each building once stood in Spina.

The first place of business was a grocery store owned by Herman Nimala in 1904. [1]   Later on, as the population grew, these places of business came into existence: the Medure Store, the McCoy Saloon, a new confectionary store and a dairy that was operated by a certain Mr. Jarvi, two clothing store, a bank and a bakery, with a "real brick and motor oven", which was the "pride and joy" of many of the townspeople. [2]   It was to this bakery that many of the house-

FOUNDATION OF TOWN BAKERY

wives would go for their supplies of bulk yeast and delicious French bread that was baked there. Many of Spina's buildings eventually were moved to Buhl and Kinney.

Water for the village was pumped from the Kinney Mine and hydrants were set up on each corner from which the householders carried their daily suplies of water for home use.

There was a volunteer fire

FIRE HYDRANTS OF SPINA

1. Wadd, John C. "Time Puts a Heavy Hand on the Once Thriving Village of Spina", Duluth News Tribune, August 8, 1951

2. Ibid.

MEDURE GROCERY

department and it operated with hand drawn equipment.

The first school in the community was a one-story affair and is today a private residence in Buhl. The second school had two stories and was known as the Hartley School. It was operated as a segment of the Buhl-Kinney School System. [3]

Although the story of Spina is a short one as far as time span is concerned, it is an interesting one. It seems that Spina had a rival in the near-by community of Kinney which was also assuming the proportions of a village in those years. The two villages were so close that it was inevitable that one should attempt to swallow up the other. At the same time, Spina was struggling against a "mine dump" which inched nearer the Village with each additional ton of overburden.

The Spina story began with a long hard fight for incorporation. The first petition for a

KINNEY MINE

3. Van Brunt, Walter, Duluth and St. Louis County Minnesota, (Chicago and New York) 1921, Vol. II

village was started in September, 1909, by Alex Renlund, Luigi Cordileone, and Fred Erickson. [4] The petition called for four hundred and fifty acres of land to be brought into the limits of the town. The petition was received by the St. Louis County Commissioners at their November, 1909, meeting "at the restaurant of Louis Cordileone." [5] At that time it was said that there were two hundred and twenty-two people living in the Village. [6] Before the election was held, however, the County Commissioners reconsidered their resolution ordering an election and withdrew their approval of the petition.

The second attempt at incorporation was presented to the St. Louis County board of Commissioners on January 4, 1910.[7] This petition called for three hundred and sixty acres of land, twenty of which would become the actual town site. The board took no action an this until October 7, 1910, when an election to incorporate was held. With a vote of thirty-three out of fifty-two against, the proposition was defeated again. [8] There was no farther attempt at incorporation until August 26, 1913, when Luigi Cordileone once again presented a petition calling for twenty acres of land to be incorporated as the Village of Spina. The people of Kinney at this time presented another petition to in-

---

4. Wadd, op. cit.

5. Ibid.

6. Van Brunt, op. cit.

7. Ibid.

8. Wadd, op. cit.

corporate both the area of Spina and Kinney as one Village to be
known as Kinney. This meant that now there were two petitions
before the St. Louis County Board of Commissioners. Luigi Cordileone's persistence paid off, for this time the Board granted
an election to be held on Cordileone's petition. Voting took
place on October 10, 1913, "in a vacant store building, lot 17,
block 3, townsite Spina." [9] When the ballots were counted, Spina had officially become a town.

It was located next to
the ore dump of the Dean
mine, and when World War I
began and the United States
became involved, the demand
for steel increased and a
stir in mining activities
also escalated operation of
the Dean. The mine "dump"
began growing and soon parts

MR. SQUILLACE

of it were washing into residential properties. A section of the
dump caved in and the Finnish Hall had to be moved. [10] Some residents were also forced to move. [11]

After 1920, Spina declined quickly. [12] Other mines had opened

---

9. Wadd, op. cit.

10. Squillace, Joseph, Spina resident from 1905-19__, interview of
    June 1963 and July 1963

11. Wadd, op. cit.

12. Ibid.

up on the Mesabi and many "Spinaites" moved to be closer to their work. Simultaneously, mining activities around Spina slowed, and its people moved away by two's and three's leaving many houses vacant and unwanted. As time went on, more and more people left, and the streets of their "one time home town" were forgotten.

Aside from the Tuck and Squillace homes, only a few weather-beaten buildings remain to verify to the passer-by that Spina is now a Ghost Town.

C. VILLAGE OF COSTIN

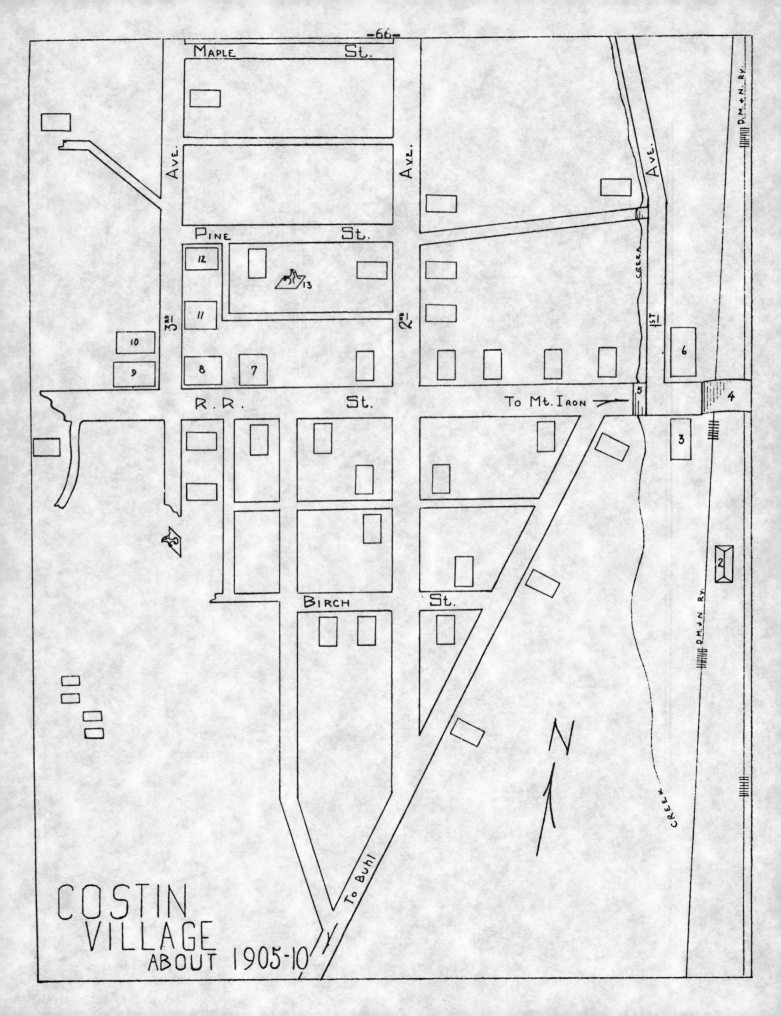

MAPLE ST.

AVE.

AVE.

PINE ST.

12

11

3ᴿᴰ

10

9

8

7

CREEK

AVE.

1ˢᵀ

2ᴺᴰ

13

6

R. R. ST.

To Mt. Iron →

5

3

4

P.M.&N. Ry.

BIRCH ST.

To Buhl

D.M.&N. Ry.

2

CREEK

N

COSTIN
VILLAGE
ABOUT 1905-10

KEY TO MAP OF COSTIN VILLAGE

1. Mayor's shacks (occupied by bachelors)

2. Mountain Iron depot (built in 1893 and razed in 1965)

3. Oliver Iron Mining Company warehouse

4. Auto and foot bridge over D.M. & N. RR tracks

5. Auto and foot bridge over creek

6. Oliver Iron Mining Company warehouse

7. Village Hall and jail

8. Skubic Saloon

9. Heikkila Saloon

10. Saloon

11. "Korkosaapas" Saloon

12. Saloon

13. One of two town wells

COSTIN VILLAGE

In section 4, of township 58-18, near what is now the town of Mountain Iron, is the site of another "ghost town" which was once known as "Costin Village."[1] John Costin, an early pioneer of Virginia, who came to the area in 1893 when Virginia was little more than a mining camp, platted the town. In 1897, along with his insurance business, he began exploring for iron ore, and gradually this enterprise began to absorb the greater part of his

JOHN COSTIN

attention. Costin Village was built as a concomitant to his substantial real-estate and fire insurance business, enterprises closely related to land speculation. Costin was also a member of the corporation which laid out the original townsite of Chisholm, the phenominal growth of which astonished the world.[2]

---

1. Van Brunt, Walter, Duluth and St. Louis County Minnesota (Chicago and New York), 1921, Vol. II

2. "An Epoch of Progress in Northern Minnesota", Illustrated Supplement to the Daily Virginian, December 3, 1915

Through business dealings he was able to obtain a tract of seventy-one acres of land near Mountain Iron. This tract was located near the Merritt's iron ore discovery and, therefore, it seemed the logical site to build a city. This acreage was originally owned by the Weyerhouser Lumber Company who sold it

EARLY DIAMOND DRILL, COSTIN

to Mr. Dave Tousignant and in turn purchased by Mr. John Costin. [3] Mr. Harvey Terrio, although a young boy at the time remembered living on property owned by Mr. Tousignant and that it was sold to Mr. Costin. His father became quite disgusted because the price of the land increased considerably after Mr. Costin purchased and platted it and he had to pay much more for the same property when soon af-

ter he decided to buy.

Veins of iron ore were known to extend from adjacent mines throughout the townsite of Mountain Iron and It was predicted that the place would be abandoned whenever the properties were fully developed. Great industrial enterprises, like those conducted in the Minnesota iron district, were not halted by trifles

3. Viitala, Matt, resident of Mountain Iron from 1906-19__, interview of July 1964

and had often been known to cause the removal or evacuation of entire towns in this and other states. No unusual, prophetic vision was required, at that time, to forecast a repetition of history, in the abandonment of the Village of Mountain Iron at some future date, when the mining companies would find it expedient to open the mines which still lie dormant beneath its surface. The oepning of such activities would create an eager demand for building sites with-

COSTIN FROM D.M. & N. TRACKS

in convenient distance of the mines and the townsite of Costin, being the only available location in that vicinity, was practically certain to become the main village of the two. [4] Mr. Costin worked many hours with J. A. Beck, John Lamminen and Dav-

id Tousignant to secure corporate powers for his newly platted Village of Costin. [5] The Village grew to a population of

MOUNTAIN IRON, 1907, FROM COSTIN

----

4.   Viitala, op. cit.

5.   Van Brunt, op. cit.

one thousand or more people and was counted among the most prosperous on the Range. [6]

Mountain Iron was a prosperous and growing community with

many fine stores
and businesses in-
cluding the Henry
Hughes and Compa-
ny (formerly the
Finnish Mercantile
Company). Hagen-

MOUNTAIN IRON, 1908, LOOKING WEST

Matchefts and Orcott Grocery and Hardware, Bill Roberts Grocery,
G. A. Apuli Hardware, Schwartz Clothing, Lasky Clothing, Charmoli

HENRY HUGHES & CO. (FORMERLY FINN. MERC.)

Meats and Grocery, Helmer Hendrickson Grocery, Bankman Clothing,
Thompson Confectionery, Andrew Saari Confectionery and Drug, D. E.
Burley Barbershop, Eilertson Restaurant, shoe repair shops, a

_____

6. Van Brunt, op. cit.

watch making and repair shop, Oakman Livery Stable, a lumber
yard, hotels Trimont, Walkers, Eilertson's McCarthy, Commer-
cial and many saloons. [7] It was, because of the closeness of

the two villages,
unnecessary for
the Costin res-
idents to devel-
op any business
enterprises since
shopping could be
easily done in
Mountain Iron.

SHOPS AND STORES IN MOUNTAIN IRON

However, Mountain Iron evidently could not satisfy the needs
of the Costinites for saloons, since they constructed five: three

of which were, the
Skubic Saloon, the
Heikkila Saloon and
a saloon known to the
residents of both
Mountain Iron and
Costin as the "Kor-
kosaapas" Saloon,
the name derived

COSTIN'S SALOONS

from the Finnish work meaning a boot with a stiff heel and sole,

7. Antilla, Mrs. Emil, resident of Costin from 1907-1961, inter-
    view of August 1964

the type worn by the owner. [8]

It was noted by all of those I interviewed that the owner of the "Korkosaapas" Saloon, known as "Korkosaapas", was found tied to his wagon at the bottom of a mine, dead from a fall involving him, his horse and wagon. It was speculated that, as he was a rich man, he was hit on the head, robbed, tied and his horse and wagon sent on its way with him in it, leading to the destruction of him, his horse, and wagon. The saloon area was a "rip-roaring", rough, tough country where there were many shootings and robberies. [9]

Early in 1900, the homes in Costin were made chiefly of tarpaper, and nothing more than shacks. An early pioneer, Mr. Matt Viitala, who came to Mountain Iron from Finland in December, 1906, remembers getting off the train at the Mountain Iron depot and the Costin area was the first to come into his view. Said Mr. Viitala, "I won't stay long in this berg." He also went on to relate, "If anyone would have told me at that time I would spend the rest of my life here, I'd have gone crazy." This was in 1906, but Mr. Viitala changed his mind as years passed.

TARPAPER HOME WITH "SILVER DOLLARS"

8. Viitala, op. cit.

9. Terrio, Mr. Harvey, resident of Costin from 1911-19__, interview of August, 1964

An interesting misnomer had spread throughout many areas of the country concerning homes on the Mesabi, and possible more in Costin, because of the great number of homes being covered with tarpaper and tin plates. Tarpaper was fastened to the outside of the house by means of round tin disks about the size of a silver dollar through which a shingling nail was driven. These disks were placed at intervals of about six to eight inches and usually three rows to a strip of tarpaper. By many it was believed that so much money was being made on the Range that people were covering their homes with tarpaper fastened with silver dollars. [10] Mr. Viitala also remembers as he was getting from the train, in 1906, how the sun shone on these tin plates, that resembled silver dollars, from many of the homes in Costin.

Costin's civic leaders made some preparation for the removal of Mountain Iron to the Costin site. A jail was erected as was a courthouse. The first Mayor was Mr. John Tim; Clerk, Martin La Plant; Trustees, George Bjornstad, Anton Cerkvenik, Joe Gagnon, Chief of Police, Charles Murphy and Lamplighter, John Berk. [11] Two main wells were dug and water was drawn from these to furnish the needs of the residents of Costin. Later, individuals sank their own wells.

Costin's residents wished to be annexed to Mountain Iron, probably to gain in and share their mineral valuation, but in-

10. Viitala, op. cit.

11. Cerkvenic, Mr. Anton, resident of Costin from 1908-1951, interview of July 1964

tended to "rule the roost." Superintendent of Mines, Mr. M. S. Hawkins and many others were against the annexation. Because of the many annexationists in the Costin area and in Mountain Iron, it was felt that if a poll were taken it would prove in favor of

Costin. Mr. Hawkinson came to Mr. Saari and told him what might happen if the people in Mountain Iron and Costin voted on the issue and asked if he would do something about it.

TYPICAL HOME STYLE, COSTIN, 1910

Mr. Saari said he would do what he could. For days, Saari campaigned throughout Mountain Iron and, because of his efforts, annexation was defeated by a small margin. [12]

Religious groups were organized to protect the morals and customs brought from points of origin. Organized in 1894, at the

TEMPERANCE SOC. IN FRONT OF 2ND FLOOR HALL

12. Saari, Mr. Andrew, resident of Mountain Iron from 1901-19__, interview of July 1964

home of Mr. and Mrs. Adolph Fernu, the Finnish Temperance Society

ORIGINAL MOUNTAIN IRON SCHOOL WHICH WAS
ATTENDED BY CHILDREN OF COSTIN

drew members from both Mountain Iron and Costin. Meetings were conducted in a hall above the Apuli Furniture and Hardware store and later in their own hall where English language training

was given to interested men of all nationalities. [13]

In 1900, thirteen hundred men were employed by the Oliver Iron Mining Company in the district, several hundred of whom worked mines in the Costin area. [14]

SECOND MOUNTAIN IRON SCHOOL (RT. PORTION
IS ORIGINAL BUILDING)

However, Mountain Iron mine was the largest and greatest producer. Others were the Snively, Hanna, Iraquois (underground)

---

13. Viitala, op. cit.

14. Ibid.

Wahcootah, Brunt (underground) and Matt.[15] Wages and hours were typical of the era. The men worked twelve hours a day from six A.M. to six P.M. for twenty cents an hour.[16]

Among the residents of Costin there were those praying for incorporation of the territory under the powers of Section 702 of the State laws of 1905. When the petition was drawn there were two hundred sixty one persons in the area involved.[17] However, when the election was held for incorporation in July, 1917, only eleven voted in favor of the incorporation. To be sure, Mountain Iron's influence was felt. Thereafter, the Village never really fully developed to its expectations. Six years later, in 1913, an attempt was made at dissolution, but failed. In January, 1915, the Village finally came to an end with the few remaining citizens voting in favor of dissolution.[18] This led to the eventual enveloping of Costin by Mountain Iron.

---

15. Wadd, Henry H. and Alm, M. R., Bulletin of the University of Minnesote, Mining Directory Issue(University of Minnesota Volume LXIV, No. 9, May 1961

16. Antilla, op. cit.

17. Van Brunt, op. cit.

18. Ibid.

D. VILLAGE OF FRANKLIN (FRANKLIN, COMMADORE, LINCOLN, HIGGINS, MINORCA AND SHAW LOCATIONS)

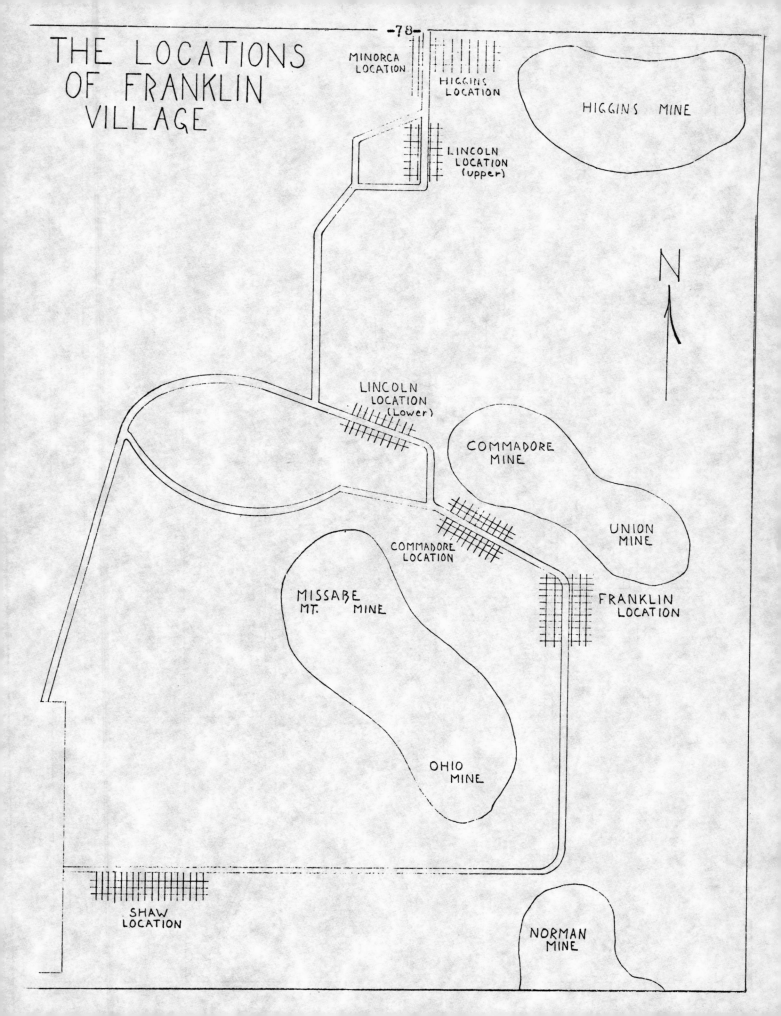

THE LOCATIONS
OF FRANKLIN
VILLAGE

MINORCA
LOCATION

HIGGINS
LOCATION

HIGGINS MINE

LINCOLN
LOCATION
(upper)

N

LINCOLN
LOCATION
(Lower)

COMMADORE
MINE

UNION
MINE

COMMADORE
LOCATION

FRANKLIN
LOCATION

MISSABE
MT. MINE

OHIO
MINE

SHAW
LOCATION

NORMAN
MINE

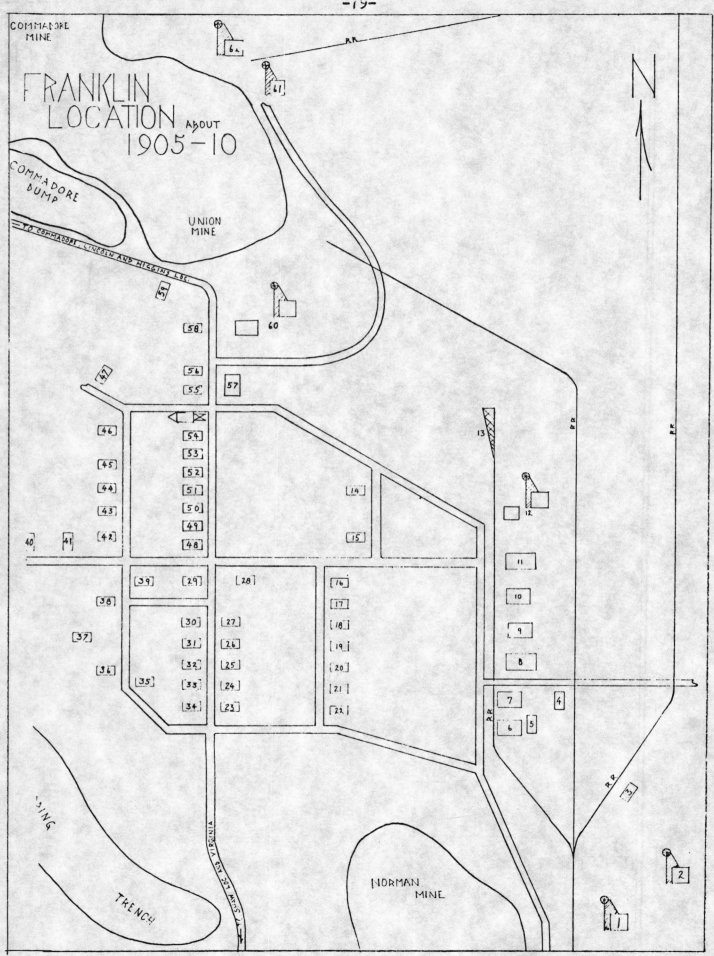

FRANKLIN
LOCATION ABOUT
1905-10

COMMADORE
LINCOLN AND
HIGGINS LOCATIONS
ABOUT   1905-1·0

MINORCA

124
123
122
121
120

CNTY. RD. NO.

119

HIGGINS

1 | 1 | 1 | 1 | 1 | 1 | 1 | 1 | 1 | 1

108

6 | 1 | 2 | 3 | 4 | 5 | 6 | 7

HIGGINS MINE

99
98
93   97
92   96
91
90   95
89
88   94
87

LINCOLN
(upper)

86

CREEK

D.M. & N. RY.

CREEK

85 | 84 | 83

LINCOLN
(lower)

COMMADORE
MINE

79
78
77

76
75
74
73

COMMADORE
DUMP

80

CREEK

71

70
69
68
67

72

TO FRANKLIN

82 | 81

SKI
JUMP
HILL

64
65
66
63

COMMADORE

TO VIRGINIA

MESABA AVE.

MISSABE MINE

MISSABE
MTN. DUMP

N

KEY TO MAP OF FRANKLIN VILLAGE (Franklin, Commadore, Lincoln, Higgins and Minorca Locations)

1. Bessemer Shaft

2. Victoria Shaft

3. Salmi

4. Gentilini

5. Vitko

6. Machine Shop

7. Blacksmith Shop

8. Carpenter Shop

9. Oil House

10. Dry House

11. Franklin Mine Office

12. Franklin Shaft and Hoist House

13. Coal Dock

14. Company Barn

15. R. Kronkite

16. Sack Boarding House

17. J. Kehoe

18. G. Lohneis

19. Buota

20. Stepich

21. Driscoll

22. Captain White

23. F. Martin

24. J. Martin

KEY TO MAP OF FRANKLIN VILLAGE (continued)

25. G. Anderson

26. Isaacson

27. Nelson

28. Doctor Miller

29. Howdu Store (Later owned by Grefenberg)

30. Marchetti

31. Turja

32. Makinen

33. Berganini

34. Sack

35. Krasaway

36. J. Maki

37. V. Makela

38. Cuppoletti

39. Grefenberg

40. Baasi

41. Boutu

42. F. Maki

43. Salmi

44. Salo

45. Mattson

46. Mannikko

47. Holmes

48. Muscatello

49. Salo

KEY TO MAP OF FRANKLIN VILLAGE (Continued)

50. Ritchie

51. Maki

52. Pennoncello

53. Campbell

54. Lahti

55. Forti

56. Swedish

57. Franklin School

58. B. Eddy

59. Oja

60. Union Shaft

61. Commadore Shaft

62. Lincoln Shaft

63. Hautala

64. Haavisto

65. Lammi

66. Salminen

67. Olson

68. Stone

69. Jenings

70. O'Neill

71. Captain and George Dickenson

72. Buotu

73. Jackson

KEY TO MAP OF FRANKLIN VILLAGE (Continued)

74. Sterle

75. Hlaca

76. Halunen

77. Salmi

78. Williamson

79. Urban

80. Lindquist

81. Sippola

82. S. Koskela

83. Tini

84. Gianlorenzi

85. Zadra

86. Village Hall

87. Hodge

88. Gilbert

89. Benkusky

90. Kishel

91. Mestnik

92. Rozniak

93. Hendy

94. Superintendent Sincock

95. Higgins School

96. Dellago

97. Hansen

98. V. Maki

99. J. Bertolas

KEY TO MAP OF FRANKLIN VILLAGE (Continued)

100. Weaver

101. Cudmore

102. Pierotto

103. Paciotti

104. Vrtachnik

105. Trebilcock

106. Santelli

107. Askew

108. Dry House for Higgins Mine

109. Village Pump

110. Skarp

111. P. Matkovich

112. P. Nordi

113. Chilcote

114. Glumack

115. Airisto

116. Carlson

117. R. Heiska

118. Rykinen

119. Water Tank for Higgins and Lincoln

120. Rinel

121. Thompson

122. Richnofsky

123. Rajala

124. Koskela

FRANKLIN VILLAGE

(Commadore, Lincoln, Higgins,
Minorca, Shaw and Franklin Locations)

A study of the plat of Franklin indicates a sizable village, the rise and decline of which follows the usual pattern. Its birth was recorded in the Virginia Enterprise on February 5, 1915, after the County Commissioners in a meeting held in January voted favorably granting corporate powers and read:

> ...Virginia is to have a brand new neighbor. It is the Village of Franklin composed of territory in the vicinity that will include the Higgins, Franklin, Norman, Commadore, Lincoln, Minorca and Shaw Locations....[1]

The original charter for incorporation had been granted the Village as early as 1895, but allowed to lapse.[2] In February, 1915, a petition had been circulated by George Lohneis, Joseph Hendy, George Noyes, Frank Kishel and others among the registered voters in the district requesting the County Commissioners to consider a special election on organization. The election was held on Tuesday, March 6, 1915 in the Franklin mine office. A census

GEORGE LOHNEIS, 1ST MAYOR OF
FRANKLIN VILLAGE

1. "Virginia Is To Have A Brand New Neighbor", Virginia Daily Enterprise, February 5, 1915

2. Ibid.

carefully taken of the people living on the land for which corporate powers had been granted, disclosed that, between January 26th and February 2nd, 1915, there were 908 residents. [3] Of the seventy votes cast, sixty-five were in favor, and five against. [4] The assessed valuation of this newly formed Village was $12,000,000. [5]

For some time these Locations sought to have a voting precinct in their territory. Because they were required to travel all the way to Gilbert or Eveleth to vote, and had no representation on the town board of supervisors and because of the distance from the township seat of government, the transaction of public business affecting them was inconvenient and variously complicated. [6]

As was the case with all communities of the Iron Ranges, the history of Franklin Village's Locations is directly related to iron mining. The "red gold" was found in the Virginia area and the rich ore which lay just beneath the topsoil was mined, giving rise to the increased number of workers and homes.

Van Brunt, in looking back over those years of the late 1800's when iron ore was first discovered, tells us:

> ...Among the early explorers of the Mesabi, those that are known to have passed over and noted the Virginia "loop" and suspected its mineral value in the 'eighties,

---

3. Van Brunt, Walter, Duluth and St. Louis County Minnesota (Chicago and New York), 1921, Vol. II

4. Ibid.

5. Ibid.

6. Virginia Enterprise, op. cit.

were members of the Merritt family, David T. Adams, and John McCaskill....It is hardly possible now to decide who was the first to begin actual explorations, in the way of test-pit sinking. One record indicates that, "the first exploratory work (in the Virginia group) was done on the Ohio" by a company in which Dr. Fred Barrett, of Tower, Thomas H. Pressnell, of Duluth, and others were interested.... "the first pit in ore in this township....was sunk on the southeast quarter, northeast quarter section 8, by Captain Cohoe, and discovered ore at a depth of thirteen feet." This was in March, 1892, and was the Missabe Mountain mine. [7]

Not all felt that the first ore discovered in the Virginia district was at the Missabe Mountain mine which was on Virginia's eastern boundary. David T. Adams writes:

...In the winter of 1890-91 I made a trip into township 58-17 in the interests of Humphreys and Atkins and myself, and camped for ten days on section 4... north and east of the present city of Virginia. During my ten days in that township I located every deposit of ore in the Virginia hills from the Alpena and Sauntry...down to the Auburn...and I brought back the minutes with the deposits well marked, including the minutes of the lands where Virginia now stands.... In the spring of 1891 I engaged the services of John Owens, (first mayor of Tower), to erect exploring camps ...now the Commadore which was the first exploration camp built in township 58-17....Exploration on this property ensued, with John Owens in charge of the men, and in the second test-pit, of a series which I had located to be sunk, the first ore in this township was discovered. A little later I discovered ore... now the Lincoln mine.
The next discovery in that township was made by the Merritt Brothers...now the Missabe Mountain mine and the next discovery was by me...now the Lonejack.... [8]

After the discovery of iron ore, test pits soon dotted the area of the Mesabi from Mountain Iron to Biwabik. Mining camps cropped up here and there and some soon developed into towns and

_____

7. Van Brunt, op. cit.

8. Ibid.

UNDERGROUND SHAFT, UNION MINE

cities. Mining equipment became as common as logging equipment. Virginia's early mines were all underground and not until the open pit mines were in operation did great numbers of miners actually come onto the scene.

Franklin, the oldest underground mine, was shored completely with hand hewn logs, doweled and dovetailed. [9] Hanson Eve Smith, a mining official for the New England Mining Company, with an office in Fargo, North Dakota, wrote of the Franklin mine:

...July 25, 1893. The Franklin mine near Virginia, James Corrigan property, (Corrigan, McKinney and Company) made its first shipment over the Duluth and Iron Range last Saturday....Ten cars were loaded the first day and the ore is very heavy, running about twenty-five tons to a car. When Superintendent C. H. Whitfork took charge of the property last winter, he made assertion that he could put the mine into shape to ship 100,000 tons this season if the owners so desire, and it appears that he has made good his word, although it is doubtful that over 50,000 tons will be shipped in 1893. [10]

The Commadore mine, first known as the New England, was test-pitted in 1892 and soon after, mined. [11] The Higgins mine, owned

---

9. Crasaway, John, resident of Franklin Location from 1900-1942, interview of August, 1965

10. Van Brunt, op. cit.

11. Ibid.

by the Oliver Iron Mining Company, in 1897, employed few men because
of the difficulty in mining operations:

> ...The mining was somewhat more difficult that at some
> other mines, at the Missabe Mountain, for instance....
> The surface was stripped and the mining carried on both
> by milling and by steam shovel, although owning to the
> steep grade, the ore mined by steam shovel was not tak-
> en direct from the mine but dumped through a shute, and
> then hoisted in the shaft....The first shipments from
> the Higgins were made in 1904. [12]

COMMADORE MINE AND LOCATION

The Lincoln-Interstate mine was begun in 1900 by the Interstate
Mining Company but no ore was shipped until 1902. [13] By 1907,
the mine had developed to a degree where four shafts had been
sunk. In 1905, Coons Pacific Mining Company started stripping
for a new open pit called the Union mine. [14] Franklin, Commadore,
Norman, Union, Bessemer, Higgins and Lincoln mines were soon deep
holes in the earth. Hundreds of men were employed and dwellings
for their families were built on leased land in the vicinity of

_____

12. Van Brunt, op. cit.

13. Ibid.

14. Crasaway, op. cit.

the mines.

Franklin, the largest of the locations in the vicinity, in 1905, had about forty-five homes, several Company buildings and a school. The Location was directly east of Virginia high atop the Virginia Hills.

Commadore Location, a half mile northeast of Franklin, had only eighteen to twenty homes. Fire destroyed several of these homes in 1918;

"VIRGINIA HILLS" LATER CALLED "FRANKLIN HILLS"

the remaining homes were removed shortly after, to lots in Virginia and surrounding area. [15] Lincoln Location originated in 1892 in the area of the Lincoln mine, and had thirteen homes. It was here that the Higgins school was built. Higgins Location with seventeen homes and four Company buildings was probably the most attractive of all the Village Locations. Tree-Lined

HIGGINS SCHOOL IN LINCOLN LOCATION, 1910

———————————————

15. Crasaway, op. cit.

boulevards and side-
walks bordered the
streets giving it
a well-groomed ap-
pearance. The yards
were large, with
fences enclosing
lawns and gardens.

HIGGINS WATER TANK, MINORCA IN FOREGROUND

By 1903, twenty-two homes had been built. Minorca Location, consisting of only five homes, lay directly west of Higgins, just a-
cross County Road number seven. The small Minorca mine, which
was begun around 1910, lay a short distance north of the small
Location and therefore its name.

Every home had boarders and the women of the household worked
constantly cleaning, washing clothes and preparing lunch pails.
In winter, during the early 1900's, a kettle was kept on the
stove to melt the snow, it being the only source of water. On a
cold winter morning, a thick layer of frost would be found on the
ceiling, caused by the warm breath of the boarders and the rest
of the family. Because of the abundance of deer and moose, it
was not unusual to see moose and deer meat on the table in season and out. [16]

No stores were developed in Franklin except for the Howdu
Confectionery which was built out of the front of the Howdu home

---

16. Crasaway, op. cit.

where residents usually bought tobacco, candy, newspapers and other small items. The store was taken over by the Herman Grefenberg family in 1914 and operated by them until 1919. [17]

Shopping was done in the busiest little city of Virginia, and in that day deliveries made it possible. Burnetti Meats and Grocery, Virginia Mercantile, Italian Work People and the Virginia Co-op all provided delivery service.

Virginia was located in a valley surrounded by a range of hills, on the Northern side by the Laurentian Highland Divide and on the east by land owned by Franklin Rockefeller. These hills became known as the "Franklin Hills". Two lakes, connected by a small channel were at the valley floor and the area round the lake was little more than a swamp with cattails and spruce. [18] Many homes were built on stilts which kept them high and dry all year except when the water rose during the spring thaw. [19]

The view from the Franklin Location toward Virginia in 1898 was described by Mr. George Anderson in our interview:

> ...Chestnut Street was about the only real street you could see. The rest were just trails. Buildings were on both sides of Chestnut Street from Shaw to the lake. Houses were scattered north and south of the main street and much timber separated the homes. A small saw mill, owned by Finnlayson and Company of St. Paul, was on the lake. The D. M. and N. had a depot on the east side of the

17. Anderson, George, resident of Franklin Location from 1900-1947, interview of July, August, 1965

18. Ibid.

19. Ibid.

main street next to the Shaw location. The city was a
mess for a long time.... [20]

Wooden sidewalks, three feet high, ran along the main street.

VIRGINIA'S "ALL BRICK" MAIN STREET ABOUT 1910

VIRGINIA'S MESABA AVENUE,
LOOKING NORTH (ABOUT 1910)

directly east up to the top of the hill and on into Franklin Lo-
.tion. Disasterous fires in 1893 and 1900 leveled most of the

_____

20. Anderson, op. cit.

city. Families in Shaw and Franklin feared the quickly spreading
fire would soon engulf their property: some had prepared for the
worst by gathering all available water in buckets and tubs. [21]
The Daily Virginian, August, 1907, reviewing the second fire,
wrote:

> ...From the time when Virginia became incorporated as
> a city, up to 1900, the city enjoyed unrivalled pros-
> perity. New mines were constantly being developed to-
> gether with the older and larger ones. Two saw mills
> were in operation, and many other minor industries had
> now gained a firm foothold in the town.
>   But, just at this time, when Virginia's future
> seemed brightest than it ever had been before, a sec-
> ond fire destroyed the main business district of the
> city, June 7, 1900. Through carelessness in handling
> the shavings burner at the old Moon and Kerr mill, a
> blaze was started which, in a short time, had the whole
> sawmill in flames. The day was very hot and everything
> as dry as it could possible be. This, together with a
> strong wind, carried the flames directly toward the
> town, and when one of the many sparks fell on the city,
> the work of destruction had begun. At sunset, there
> was nothing left of it but one vast space of smoulder-
> ing ruin.... [22]

Hospital facilities were also available only in Virginia, but
early mining doctors Malmgres, Sheely, Ewens and Malmstrom maintained a clinic in a large Company home which had been renovated
for their use. This clinic was in the Shaw Location just across
the street from the D.M.& N. tracks. Miners paid one dollar for
hospitalization and clinic "out-patient" service. [23]

---

21. Anderson, op. cit.

22. A review of the Second fire in Virginia, "Virginian", Virginia,
Minnesota, August, 1907

23. Gentilini, Secundo, resident of Franklin Location from 1911-1946,
interview of August, 1965

When the Franklin School closed, the children attended the Central School in Virginia. Early teachers were Miss Hende, Mrs. Beach, Miss Homis and Miss Irene who, it was said, was walking home at dusk from the school, down the long hill to Lincoln Location and was

FRANKLIN SCHOOL, 1915

held up by a young man with a revolver. He demanded her money or he'd shoot. Her reply, "Go ahead and shoot." Surprised by her retort, he fled, only to be caught later. [24] Hay rides and winter sleigh ride parties were quite frequent. A teacher would accompany fifteen to twenty children on the outing and the destination would usually be Ely Lake just south of Eveleth.

Along side the school, the men of the Location would build a skating rink which was used and enjoyed by all the residents. Winter weekends and evenings usually would not pass without seeing sledders by the score slipping down the road from the top of Franklin Location all the way down to Commadore, a distance of close to

24. Gentilini, op. cit.

a mile. [25] Many skiers got their ski legs on "Ski Jump Hill," a
mine dump that was shaped perfectly for a jump and landing.

In summer, the horse drawn beer wagons would make their
daily trips through the Locations selling their product for ten
cents a quart. The frequent patrons were the miners who quenched
their thirsts from the contents of these wagons.

No police protection came to the Locations until they incorporated. Mr. Bill Sanski was the first constable. [26] Captain
White, big, fat and mean, was an early mining captain, and a
threat by mom to her misbehaving youngster of, "I'll go and tell
Captain White," was usually enough to straighten him out. [27] A
9:00 P.M. curfew, located in Higgins, sounded each evening, and
come this siren, you'd better be off the street. [28] Constable
Sanski's biggest chore, it seemed, was to help the drunks, who
would return from Virginia after dark, find their home and prevent them from falling over the neighbor's cow that could be
found just about anywhere. [29]

Churches never having been built in the Locations, the school
house was used for Sunday school where classes were conducted for

25. Bergdahl, Helmi, resident of Commadore Location from 1906-1920,
     interview of August, 1965

26. Gentilini, op. cit.

27. Ibid.

28. Nakari, Violet, resident of Commadore Location from 1909-1918,
     interview of August, 1965

29. Gentilini, op. cit.

all denominations by Captain Briggs of Virginia's Salvation Army.
These classes, led later by other Army members, continued for
quite a few years. [30]   Those families who were church goers, be-
longed to a parish in Virginia and for many of the earliest years,
walked.

Franklin Village built a pump station and laid water lines
between Higgins and Franklin at the cost of $50,000 only to find
the water unusable. [31]   Underground water was then found near the
Higgins mine and for years this was the source of water for the
entire Village. [32]   On December 17, 1917, an election was held
to decide whether to erect a waterworks for the Village, for
public and private use, the cost not to exceed $60,000. [33]   Twen-
ty voted, all in favor. [34]   In the summer an all metal water tank
was erected and a pump station was built near the Higgins Location. [35]   Running water in the home made it possible for Franklin
to gain the reputation of being a well administrated Village with
many of the conveniences of larger communities. [36]

----

30.   Gentilini, op. cit.

31.   Trebilcock, Sam, resident of Lincoln Location from 1912-1940
      interview of August, 1965

32.   Ibid.

33.   Ibid.

34.   Van Brunt, op. cit.

35.   Trebilcock, op. cit.

36.' Van Brunt, op. cit.

The diggings of the mines started eating away at the Franklin Hills to a point where in 1942 the residents were asked to leave. By 1948, they were all gone. Franklin Location's steel

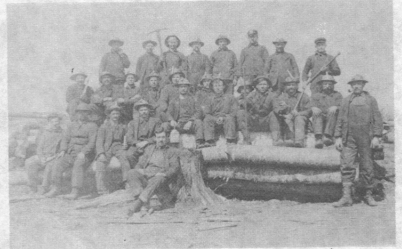

water tank, its last structure to be moved, was transported to Midway Gardens where it is still in use.[37] Higgins curfew tower remained in operation until

UNDERGROUND MINERS, (NOTE CANDLES)

1950 and was missed by all who became accustomed to its siren at 8:00 A.M., noon and 9:00 P.M. A water tank, erected in 1925 across from Minorca Location, was recently torn down. Higgins was the last of the Village Locations to be moved, with the exception of Shaw, which is still in existence as Franklin Village. The Missabe Mountain mine operations had expanded to a point where two blocks of the Location were removed, leaving twelve of the original twenty-four homes. On August 14,1957, the Village Hall, which had been in Lincoln Location, was sold, and an abandoned building in the Shaw became the meeting house.[38] Present officers of Franklin Village are: Mayor, Matt Fabish; Clerk, Mrs. Helen Skarp; Constable, Mr. Norman Revaard; Trustees, Kenneth Larks and John Spo-

37. Mesabi Daily News, (Photograph of tank being moved), Virginia, Minnesota, November, 1948

38. Trebilcock, op. cit.

larish;   Treasurer, Frank Klima;   Attorney, Jerry Ketola. [39]

As we stand in Shaw Location and look at the remains of the Franklin Hills toward the once existing Franklin, Commadore, Lincoln, Higgins and Minorca Locations, it is difficult to imagine that hundreds of people once lived there. Large gaping holes have been dug and as one connects the other, the result is one great abyss as a reminder of the tons of earth removed and a hint of the task men and machines endured. Franklin Village's losses were Virginia's gain as most villagers moved into the "Queen City."

---

39. Skarp, Helen, clerk of present Franklin Village, interview of July, 1965

-V-

THE INTER-URBAN ELECTRIC LINE

INTER-URBAN ELECTRIC ROUTE
1912 - 1927

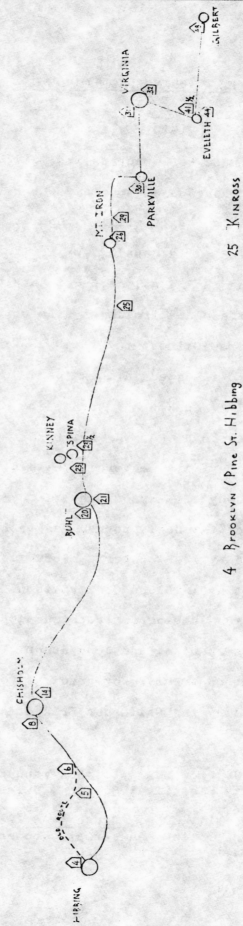

St. Louis County

4   Brooklyn (Pine St. Hibbing)
5   Kitzville
6   Mitchell
8   Albany
14 Myers
20 D.M. & N. Depot (Buhl)
21 Sharon
23 Lucknow
23½ Kinney - Spina

25 Kinross
26 Mt. Iron
29½ Brunt
30 Mud Lake Road (Parkville)
31 Virginia (North Side)
32 Virginia (Wyoming Ave.)
41½ West Eveleth
44 East Eveleth
45 Gilbert

◇ - STATION AND NUMBER

INTER-URBAN ELECTRIC LINE

The Mesabi Range in 1910 was a beehive of activity: thousands were employed and there were many cities, villages and locations. Transportation, in those days, was inadequate. Automobiles were few, with the horse and buggy still a popular means of transportation: "old dobbin" could usually get you to your destination. A few wealthy men on the Range, in Duluth and in the East saw financial possiblities in a trolley system connecting Range cities and locations from Gilbert to Hibbing. Prominent men on the Range and Duluth who invested in this public utility included W. P. Chinn, Samuel J. Cusson, Richard Chinn, Dr. F. H. McIntyre, John D. Lamont, Chester H. Rogers, Dr. Dana C. Rood and Albert B. Coates. [1] They, along with Eastern investors, were financed by the Tucker and Anthony Company of Boston. [2]

The property of the newly formed Mesaba Railway Company was built and developed by the Webster Construction Company, an Eastern concern, with the Cleveland Construction Company of Cleveland, Ohio, as sub-contractor for construction of over-head lines, power house and sub-station, and John Runquist Construction Company of Duluth, sub-contractor for grading. [3] The necessary bridges were constructed by the Gallagher Bridge and Construction Com-

1. Bergeson, Mr. J. O., an unpublished manuscript, property of the St. Louis County Historical Society, Duluth, n. d.

2. Massingham, Mr. William S., Sketches of Mesabi Range Towns, an unpublished handwritten manuscript, property of the Minnesota Historical Society, St. Paul, n.d.

3. Bergeson, op. cit.

pany. [4]   These bridges were located at Sparta, Eveleth, Thomas

Addition and in Virginia at Bailey's Mill and the Oliver shops.

The last bridge on the line was in Lucknow.

Surveying had begun in 1911, and in July, a year later, the

first rails were laid. [5] Mr. J. O. Bergeson, auditor and assis-

tant treasurer, wrote about that Christmas Eve Day:

> ...That twenty-fourth day of December in 1912 was a
> big and important day for Range towns, and it was the
> beginning of the end of livery stables, horses and
> buggies. In Virginia there had been four large livery
> stables on the Chestnut Street...other fine business
> establishments now take their place.... [6]

William Massingham in his "Sketches of Mesabi Range Towns",

tells of the railway's importance to the Range:

> ...The beginning of operations on this, the first
> electric road on the Minnesota Iron Range, marked
> an important and interesting period of its history.
> The rapidly increasing population and multiplying
> of cities and villages have made this means of trans-
> portation a necessity, and the sight of the first e-
> lectric cars was a great event especially to many who
> had not lived in a country supplied with these modern
> wonders. [7]

> ...The cars were packed t   .rst two days with
> people of all the many n   .alities of the Range,
> eager to ride on the new .d handsome cars of the
> first electric road of the Mesaba Range.... [8]

The first car left the car house which was located on Vir-

ginia's "North Side", and parked in front of the depot on Wyo-

---

4. Bergeson, op. cit.

5. Ibid.

6. Ibid.

7. Massing   , op. cit.

8. Ib'.

ming Avenue, now Third Avenue, at 4:45 A.M., with throngs of
cheering and excited Virginians who were about to witness the
introduction of the Range's electric transportation system. [9]
The eight mile trip from Virginia to Gilbert got under way
at five A.M. sharp. [10] On this, the first run by the new line,
a Finn had paid the first fare of twenty cents. [11]

> ...The conductor on this first trip was a Swede,
> Mr. A. Matson. The motorman, Peter Martinson, was
> also a Swede. Like most of the conductors and
> motormen, these young men had been employed on
> the street car system of Duluth and Superior. Mr.
> C. W. Kenny acted as pilot over the new track. [12]

On December 25, 1912, two hour service was inaugurated between Gilbert and Buhl. Because of popular demand, additional
lines were soon laid from Buhl to Hibbing with six cars giving
regular hourly service. By 1913 this same hourly service was
accomplished with only four cars.

Headquarters for the Company were in Virginia's "North Side"
where a large car barn, attached office and paint shop were located. Electric power for the cars came from a powerhouse near
the Rainy Lake Lumber Company saw mill site.

City and county officials assembled in the various towns on
the Mesaba Range through which this new service was being inaugurated to honor and pay their respects to the introduction of what
was then the modern type passenger service. Modern indeed, as

9. Bergeson, op. cit.

10. Ibid.

11. Massingham, op. cit.

12. Ibid.

INTER-URBAN'S ELECTRIC CAR, PETE VOLDEN (CENTER)

described by Mr. J. O. Bergeson:

> ...high speed electric steel cars, forty feet in
> length seating capacity 48....hot water heated and
> with smoking and baggage compartments and toilet
> facilities....the car bodies were built for protection
> in extreme cold weather during the winter, being
> equipped with double side walls sheathed outside
> with one-eighth inch by thirty-four inch steel plate,
> corked insulated and removeable storm sash. The in-
> terior finish was dark oak with white ceiling and
> forty watt lights over each seat making it possible
> to read without eye strain....[13]

During all the years of operation the Company maintained an

eighteen hour passenger service schedule and had a payroll aver-

aging 140 employees. [14] Mr. Berguson provided a list of those

he remembered in the employment of the line from its inception

until its death:

_____

13. Bergeson, op. cit.

14. Ibid.

INTERIOR OF ELECTRIC CAR

...George Mattocks, ticket and freight agent: Ed Norsted, in the accounting department: George A. Schultz,
fireman in the railway power house: Siguard Copperud,
who acted in the capacity of conductor, motorman and
train dispatcher: Vaino Saranen and John Lahti, both
section foreman: Mrs. Dorothy Gish Pengrey, stenographer: Guy R. Golden, served in the capacities of conductor, motorman, dispatcher and station agent: Thomas
Graham, motorman: Fred Brown, in charge of overhead
lines: Karl A. Evenson, motorman: Wm. J. Luke, station
agent at Eveleth, and Gilbert: Joseph H. Angellar, station at Eveleth for many years: Harry Cohen, was station
agent at Mountain Iron for years: Herbert Forder and C.
Crosby, were agents in Buhl: Miss Hannah Bloomquist,
stenographer in the accounting department: Carl Nygaard,
George F. Anderson, Frank R. Hall, August F. Ilse, were
machinists in the carhouse: Oscar and Barney Buvarp, car
painters: W. Erickson, conductor: Herman Frajola, station agent at Gilbert: Hjalmer Niemi, agent at Genoa:
R. H. Moore, agent in Virginia: A. E. Eddy, station agent
in Mountain Iron: N. E. Supry, agent in Lucknow: J. A.
Frey, agent in Chisholm: Mary Oberstar, agent in Kitzville: Ed Burdash, agent in Hibbing: Oliver Hale, agent
in Virginia (North Side): Maurice Kirby, assistant agent
in Virginia (North Side): Gust Erickson, conductor and
motorman: Carl B. Larson, an electrician during the con-

struction of the line, later became conductor: Arnold
Hawkinson, timekeeper: J. O. Bergeson, head time keeper
during construction and later auditor and assistant
treasurer: Wm. McLeod, cashier: Harry A. Montieth,
dispatcher: Peter Volden, one of the first motorman:
Wm. Jamieson, conductor: J. P. Brady, conductor: H. S.
Newton, first manager of the line, came from Connecticut
with his family and was relieved of his duties in December, 1914, followed by R. W. Reynolds who was in turn
relieved by L. W. Hayes in January, 1913....[15]

On November 26, 1913, an explosion from a hot air heater in
one of the cars started a fire which consumed the car barn, office
and cars numbered thirteen, fifteen, sixteen, seventeen, eighteen,
one hundred one and seven. [16]   Fortunately, they were covered by
insurance and by June of 1914
all cars except number seven were
replaced. [17]   Later, in that
same year another car was
destroyed by fire as it sat
outside of the barn. Again it
was determined that a faulty
stove caused the fire. The new
car house was built with a more

RE-BUILT CAR HOUSE AND OFFICE

fire-proof concrete roof. To prevent the possibility of the office
and its pertinent records again being destroyed by fire, a new general
office building was erected several yards west of the car house.

---

15. Bergeson, op. cit.

16. Ibid.

17. Ibid.

For several years the electric railway was very prosperous.
As mining operations increased, so did the population and this
was the premise on which the investors relied.

On April 7, 1914, the Mesaba Railway Company entered agreement with W. H. Newbolds Sons and Company, Section three of said
agreement reads as follows:

> ...The Railway Company covenants and agrees that so
> long as any bonds issued or to be issued under its
> said mortgage shall remain outstanding, it will each
> year set aside from its gross earnings a sum equiv-
> alent to at least fifteen per centum (15%) therefore,
> which shall be used for no other purpose than the
> maintenance of the properties of the Railway Company....[18]

Soon after that time the Company paid its first dividends
amounting to $42,475. Dividends were paid each year thereafter
until October 1, 1917. [19]

An interview with Mr. Peter Volden, the oldest motorman and
conductor with the line gave several interesting incidents relating to his job with the Company:

> ...Fares in the beginning, were ten cents to Eveleth,
> twenty cents to Gilbert, Parkville five cents, Mountain
> Iron ten cents and Hibbing fifty cents....The cars
> often reached speeds up to forty miles per hour and
> there were times when people, cars, trucks, cows, chick-
> ens and even other trollies got in the way, the end re-
> sult sometimes spelling disaster....demerits would be
> issued to the conductor for taking the car from the
> barn without a cow catcher....when the barn burned, the
> dispatcher had to stand outside in the wet snow while
> waiting for fire fighting equipment to arrive....In
> days when many cities were dry, during early prohibi-
> tion, the railway was the most expedient way to go for
> a bottle in Buhl, or wherever one could buy it. Quite
> often the "Feds" would stop the car, enter, and begin

---

18. Olson, Russell L., materials relating to street railway collec-
    tions, Minnesota Historical Society, St. Paul, n.d.

19. Ibid.

a thorough search of the car and its passengers.
More than one bottle hung out of the window by a
string during those searches....The stations, most
of them being small candy stores or sometimes confectionery stores, were good targets for robbers
and quite frequently the agent was forced to relin-
quish his cash....[20]

An article from the Virginia Enterprise described one such

robbery attempt:

...Near-robbery at Mountain Iron Station....H. Cohen,
who is in charge of the Mesaba Railway Company station at Mountain Iron, was the near victim of a robbery at the station last Tuesday. A would-be robber
pried open a window and tried to enter, but Cohen's
shrieks and cries frightened him away. The prowler
was not masked....[21]

Hints for a new conductor was put out by A. P. Paulson and

were as follows:

...1.   Always keep the same amount of change in the
        changer from day to day.
   2.   Silver dollars in the left front trouser pocket
   3.   Register key and switch key right front pocket
   4.   Currency in trouser watch pocket
   5.   Pencils, upper right vest pocket
   6.   Coupons, lower left vest pocket
   7.   Watch, upper right vest pocket
   8.   Half dollars, lower right coat pocket
   9.   Hat checks, lower left coat pocket
  10.   Tickets, middle left coat pocket
  11.   Punch, middle right coat pocket
  12.   Unfilled ticket and coupon envelopes, upper right
        coat pocket
  13.   Pass pad, upper left coat pocket
  14.   Filled ticket envelopes, upper left inside coat
        pocket
  15.   Tarriff sheet, time table and excess baggage
        checks upper right inside coat pocket [22]

---

20. Volden, Peter, employee of the Inter-Urban Electric Line from
     1912-1927, interview of August 1965

21. "Near Robbery at Mountain Iron Station", *Virginia Daily Enter-
     prise*, July, 1921

22. Bergeson, *op. cit.*

Station agents were given duties and rules by which each station was run. These duties were as follows:

> ...Open station at a certain hour (to be understood)
> Keep station clean and allow no loafers
> Keep ticket case filled so that passengers will not
> by compelled to wait until you find the tickets
> Keep cash book posted up daily and neatly
> Make all daily reports promptly
> Agent should place their signature in place provided
> on each coupon sold. [23]

The beginning of the end was slow and bitter. By 1920, good concrete highways were built and paralleled the Inter-Urban right-of-way- from end to end, and with the advent of private automobiles and unregulated bus competition, it became difficult to operate and make expenses. The Company itself invested $150,000 in bus equipment to try to gain a balance with competitors. [24] No relief was obtained in the way of transportation regulation and the Company was compelled to cease operations on April 16, 1927, thereby throwing about 150 employees out of work, a majority of whom made their homes in Virginia and nearly bankrupting several individuals. [25]

J. O. Bergeson writes of the final days of the Mesabi Electric Company:

> ...The property was placed in receivership on March
> 7, 1924, and Federal Judge William A. Cant, of Duluth, appointed Oscar Mitchell, of Duluth and James C.
> Chestnut, receivers. J. O. Bergeson, auditor and
> assistant treasurer stayed on the property until
> it was entirely sold in December, 1927....

---

23. Bergeson, op. cit.

24. Ibid.

25. Ibid.

Higgins School - was located in the Higgins Location three miles directly north of Franklin and was built in 1908 at a cost of $2,000. It had two rooms and had an eighty pupil capacity.

Franklin School - located in the Franklin Location, built in 1896 at a cost of $1500. It housed grades K-4. The first educational facility in the Virginia School District was the Central School and the Franklin School was the second.

School Farm Barn - located on the site of our golf course
clubhouse. The farm consisted of sixty-seven acres and
produced the potatoes, milk, eggs and vegetables needed for
the domestic science department and cafeteria. The dairy
cattle, horses, hogs and poultry were also used for labora-
tory problems such as judging, feeding, care and manage-
ment. Students were required to operate and repair farm
machinery.

School Farm - located on the present site of the Virginia Municipal Golf
Course. The barn sat almost exactly where the clubhouse now stands. The
home on the right was built for the Superintendent of the School Farm and
was used in more recent years as housing for some of the hospital nurs-
ing staff. A small cemetery was located in the area of the present hospital. Story has it that when the basement was dug for the Superintendent's
home, four graves were unearthed.

Central School - built in 1894 for $14,000, was located on the present site of the Holy Spirity church. It was the first school built to meet the needs of District 22. After it was no longer used as a school, the Iver Johnson Lumber Company purchased it and conducted their business there.

Bus Garage and Bus Fleet - built in 1921 later enlarged. The building is presently the Auto Technology Shop, Small Engine Repair Shop, Band Hall and Choir facility.

Technical High School - was built in 1910 at an estimated
cost of $125,000. It was later used as the Virginia Jr.
College. The Technical Vocational addition was built
during the period of 1917-1921 at a cost of $1,098,831.
It had 31 rooms, 2 gyms, a swimming pool, auditorium and
cafeteria plus a very modern Vocational Education area.

Johnson School - built in 1906 at a cost of $85,000. It
was sold in 1979 for $40,000 to the Arrowhead Economic
Opportunity Association (AEOA).

Jefferson School - built in 1924 and razed in 1967. The dome at the top of the fire escape, which was a spiral slide, was struck by lightning just prior to the start of the school day. Luckily, none of the falling bricks hit any of the children waiting at that doorway to enter the school. The dome was not replaced.

Roosevelt High School (original) - built on the present site of the Roosevelt Elementary (formerly Roosevelt High School). It was built in 1904 at a cost of $65,000 and was dismantled in 1927 to make way for the present Roosevelt building.

Horace Mann - built in 1904 with a new section being added in 1924. The building is still being used by the school district for the Alternative Education program, Early Childhood Special Education and Early Childhood Family Education.

Horace Mann - The original section, built in 1914, was called the Southside School. A new section was added in 1924 and then named Horace Mann. The building is still being used by the school district for the Alternative Education program, Early Childhood Special Education and Early Childhood Family Education.

Technical High School - built in 1910 at an estimated cost of $125,000. Other additions came around 1917. This part of the building was, for a number of years, Virginia Jr. College.

Washington School - under construction in December, 1921. The
Jefferson School can be seen three blocks north.

Lincoln School was built in 1923 after the Primary School which was located on that site was razed. The school closed in 1971 and was sold to the Trenty Law Firm in 1977.

Midway School - built in 1958 at a cost of $652,000. When student popu-lation declined, they were transported to other schools in the district. The school is being leased by ECSU and the Mesabi Family YMCA.

-VII-

BIBLIOGRAPHY

BIBLIOGRAPHY

MANUSCRIPTS AND DOCUMENTS

Berguson, J. O., an unpublished manuscript property of the St. Louis County Historical Society, Duluth Minnesota, n. d.

Chanak, George, "Farewell to Poverty and Happiness," an unpublished manuscript written of the days of Carson Lake Location, Hibbing, Minnesota, n. d.

Franklin, Village of, minutes of Village meetings, property of Village Secretary Mrs. Helen Skarp, Franklin, Minnesota, August 14 1957

Griffin, R. L., Forests and Logging in the Vicinity of Hibbing, manuscript on file in St. Louis County Historical Society, Duluth, Minnesota, 1930

Hammer, Mrs. A. S., "Personal Touches of West Eveleth and Leonidas," an unpublished document written for West Eveleth and Leonidas Civic League, property of Historian of the Civic League, Leoneth, Minnesota, n. d.

King, Franklin A., caption to front cover drawing of steam engine at Iron Junction train depot, Missabi Iron Ranger, October, 1962

Longyear, Edmund J., Reminiscences of, an unpublished manuscript property of the Minnesota Historical Society, St. Paul, Minnesota, 1951

Massingham, William S., Sketches of Mesabi Range Towns, unpublished handwritten manuscript, property of the Minnesota Historical Society, St. Paul, Minnesota, n.d.

Olson, Russel L., materials relating to street railway collections, property of Minnesota Historical Society, St. Paul, Minnesota, n.d.

Smith, Hanson Eve, Sketches of the History of mines of the Missabi Iron Ranges of Minnesota, property of the Minnesota Historical Society, St. Paul, Minnesota, n.d.

MAGAZINES, PAMPHLETS, PERIODICALS AND NEWSPAPERS

Daily Virginian, Illustrated Supplement, December 3, 1915

Daily Virginian, Industrial Edition, August 30, 1907

Eveleth News, December, 1906

Eveleth Star, March 12, 1895

Jones and Laughlin Mining Company Official, "A Tribute to Mr. E. S. Tillinghast," Engineering and Mining Journal, n.d.

Mesabi Daily News, March 24, 1956: August 8, 1951

Missabe Iron Ranger, December, 1956: September, 1962: October, 1962

Ore, Iron and Men, June, 1958

The Virginia Story, unpublished historical booklet of the Virginia Centennial celebration, Virginia Chamber of Commerce, Virginia, Minnesota, July 14-17, 1949

Thunder on the Missabe, an unpublished brochure commemorating the historic run over the rails of the Duluth Missabe and Iron Range Railroad from and to Duluth via Two Harbors, Biwabik, Iron Junction and Alborn, July, 1958

Virginia Enterprise, September 7, 1894: August 31, 1894

Virginia Enterprise, "Virginia is to Have a Brand New Neighbor," February 5, 1915

Virginia Enterprise, "Near Robbery at Mountain Iron Station," July, 1921

Wade, Henry H. and Alm, Mildred R., Bulletin of the University of Minnesota Mining Directory, Volume LXIV, Number 9, May 1, 1961

Wolff, Julius F. Jr., Vanished Settlements of the Minnesota Arrowhead Country, an unpublished pamphlet, property of the Minnesota Historical Society, St. Paul, Minnesota, n.d.

BOOKS

Gillette, Arson C., Arthur D. and Genevieve, The Marvelous Mesabi, Clark Publishing Company, Madison, Wisconsin, 1936

Van Brunt, Walter, Duluth and St. Louis County, Minnesota, (Chicago and New York) 1921, Volumes I, II

Woodbridge, Dwight E., History of Duluth and St. Louis County, C. F. Cooper and Co., Chicago, Illinois, Volume II, 1910

PHOTOGRAPHS

Iron Junction

Iron Junction, about 1905, property of Jessie Grierson, Iron Junction

Downey Hotel, property of Mrs. E. M. Moline, Iron Junction

Ten Car Coal Dock, property of Mrs. E. M. Moline, Iron Junction

Sixteen residents of Iron Junction, property of Mrs. E. M. Moline, Iron Junction

Hotel Missaba, property of Mrs. E. M. Moline, Iron Junction, Minnesota

Engine, Iron Junction Depot, 1893, property of Mrs. E. M. Moline, Iron Junction, Minnesota

Moline Grocery and Post Office, M. R. Johnson Store, Ansley Saloon, property of Mrs. E. M. Moline, Iron Junction, Minnesota

Interior of Moline Grocery, 1919, property of Mrs. E. M. Moline, Iron Junction, Minnesota

Firemen, property of Mrs. E. M. Moline, Iron Junction

County School, property of Mrs. E. M. Moline, Iron Junction

Interior, Iron Junction School, property of Mrs. E. M. Moline, Iron Junction, Minnesota

Elbow Lake and Excursion Boat, taken from The Virginia Story, unpublished historical booklet of the Virginia Centennial Celebration, Virginia Chamber of Commerce, Virginia, Minnesota, July 14-17, 1949

CARSON LAKE

The Real Carson Lake, 1903, property of Mrs. M. Cavanaugh, Kelly Lake

Hamre Grocery and Post Office, property of Mr. H. Mickelson, Kelly Lake

Leonidas

Early Steam Engine in Leonidas Switch Yard, property of Mr. Ed Mills, Eveleth

Digging of Run-off Trench, property of Mr. Ed Mills, Eveleth

Santa (Waldron Holder), Mule and Sleigh, property of Mr.
    Ed Mills, Eveleth

First School in Leonidas, property of Mr. Ed Mills, Eveleth

New Brick Structure, property of Mr. Ed Mills, Eveleth

New School with Addition (Orig. Sch. in Background) pro-
    perty of Mr. Ed Mills, Eveleth

Original Township Hall, property of Mr. Ed Mills, Eveleth

Hall As It Stands Today, taken by Rod Halunen

Hammer Groc. and P. O., property of Mrs. H. Hammer, Leoneth

Spina

Spina, 1920, From Dean Mine Dump, property of.

Foundation of Town Bakery, taken by Rod Halunen

Fire Hydrants of Spina, taken by Rod Halunen

Kedure Grocery, taken by Rod Halunen

Kinney Mine, taken from Van Brunt, Walter, Duluth and St.
    Louis County, Minnesota, (Chicago and New York), 1921,
    Volumes II

Mr. Joe Squillace, taken by Rod Halunen

Costin

John Costin, taken from the Daily Virginian, Illustrated
    Supplement, December 3, 1915

Early Diamond Drill, Costin, property of Mr. Andrew Saari,
    Mt. Iron, Minnesota

Mountain Iron, 1907, From Costin, property of Mrs. S. Anttila,
    Virginia

Mountain Iron, 1908, Looking West, property of Mrs. S. Anttila,
    Virginia

Henry Hughes and Co. (Formerly Finn. Merc.), property of Mr.
    Andrew Saari, Mt. Iron

Shops and Stores in Mountain Iron, property of Mr. Andrew
    Saari, Mt. Iron

Costin's Saloons, property of Mrs. E. Anttila, Virginia

Tarpaper, Home with "Silver Dollars", property of Mrs. E. Anttila, Virginia

Typical Home Style, Costin, 1910, property of Mrs. E. Anttila, Virginia

Temperance Soc. in Front of 2nd Floor Hall, property of Mrs. E. Anttila, Virginia

Original Mountain Iron School Which Was Attended by Children of Costin, property of Mr. Andrew Saari, Mt. Iron

Second Mountain Iron School (Rt. Portion is Original Building), property of Mr. Andrew Saari, Mt. Iron

Franklin

George Lohneis, 1st Mayor of Franklin Village, property of Mr. George Lohneis, Virginia

Underground Shaft, Union Mine, property of Mr. Sam Trebilcock, Britt, Minnesota

Commadore Mine and Location, property of Mr. Sam Trebilcock, Britt, Minnesota

"Virginia Hills" later Called "Franklin Hills", property of Mr. Sam Trebilcock, Britt, Minnesota

Higgins, School in Lincoln Location, 1910, property of Mr. Sam Trebilcock, Britt, Minnesota

Higgins Water Tank, Minorca in Foreground, property of Mrs. Ruth Gilbert, Virginia, Minnesota

Virginia's "All Brick" main Street about 1910, property of Mr. Sam Trebilcock, Britt, Minnesota

Virginia's Mesaba Avenue, Looking North, about 1910, property of Mr. Sam Trebilcock, Britt, Minnesota

Franklin School, 1915, property of Mrs. Helmi Bergdahl, Virginia

Underground Miners, (Note Candles), property of Mr. Sam Trebilcock, Britt, Minnesota

Inter-Urban Electric Line

Inter-Urban's Electric Car, Pete Volden (Center), property
of Mr. Peter Volden, Virginia, Minnesota

Interior of Electric Car, property of Mr. Peter Volden,
Virginia, Minnesota

Re-built Car House and Office, taken by Rod Halunen

PERSONAL INTERVIEWS

Iron Junction

Zacher, William, resident of Iron Junction from 1897-1909,
interview of July, 1964

Woods, Grace Zacher, resident of Iron Junction from 1897-
1923, interview of August 4, 1964

Carson Lake

Rauker, George, resident of Carson Lake Location from 1910-
1947, interview of July, 1965

Michelson, H. O., resident of Carson Lake Location from 1901-
1950, interview of July, 1965

Shubat, Charles, owner of the Northern Transportation Company,
interview of August, 1965, Hibbing, Minnesota

Leonidas

Mills, Ed, resident of Leonidas Location from 1911-1940, inter
view of July, 1965

Hammer, Hulda, resident of Leonidas Location from 1915-1920
interview of August, 1964

Peterson, Horton, resident of Leonidas Location from 1912-
1940, interview of August, 1965

Spina

Squillace, Joseph, resident of Spina from 1905-19__, interview of June, 1963 and July, 1963

Coshin

Viitala, Matt, resident of Mountain Iron from 1906-19__, inter-
    view of July, 1964

Anttila, Mrs. Emil, resident of Costin from 1907-1961, inter-
    view of August, 1964

Terrio, Harvey, resident of Costin from 1911-19__, interview
    of August, 1964

Cerkvenic, Anton, resident of Costin from 1908-1951, interview
    of July, 1964

Saari, Andrew, resident of Mountain Iron from 1901-19__, inter-
    view of July, 1964

Franklin

Crasaway, John, resident of Franklin Location from 1900-1942,
    interview of August, 1965

Anderson, George, resident of Franklin Location from 1900-1947,
    interview of July, August, 1965

Gentilini, Secundo, resident of Franklin Location from 1911-
    1946, interview of August, 1965

Bergdahl, Helmi, resident of Commadore Location from 1906-1920,
    interview of August, 1965

Makari, Violet, resident of Commadore Location from 1909-1918,
    interview of August, 1965

Trebilcock, Sam, resident of Lincoln Location from 1912-1940,
    interview of August, 1965

Skarp, Helen, clerk of present Franklin Village, interview of
    July, 1965

Inter-Urban Electric Line

Volden, Peter, employee of the Inter-Urban Electric Line from
    1912-1927, interview of August, 1965